BIKE RIDES AROUND MALMESBURY

& NORTH WILTSHIRE

Judy Jones

Blue Tree Books

First published in 2008 by
Blue Tree Books, 28 Back Hill,
Malmesbury, Wiltshire
SN16 9BT
United Kingdom

A catalogue record for this book is available from the British Library.

ISBN 978-0-9557682-1-7

Printed on recycled paper and bound in Great Britain by
CPI Antony Rowe, Chippenham, Wiltshire

CONTENTS

Acknowledgements

Grateful thanks to the friends and neighbours who got on their bikes to test out my draft routes: Bill Reed, Sue and Dave Alexander, Mark Hughes, Guy Rushton and Anna Palmer. The final text reflects their many helpful comments and suggestions for improving my early drafts. I am indebted to Mary Ray Smith (www.butterflystudio.co.uk) for creating the Title Illustration, showing the number and title of each ride and the geographical area featured in the book; to Sue Austin (www.sueaustin.co.uk) for proofreading and formatting my computer files; and to Jean Jones and Ian Christie, as always, for their support and encouragement.

Foreword

After moving from west London to Malmesbury in 1997, I made an exciting discovery – great cycling country within easy reach of my new home town. Sparsely-populated, largely flat, with a few inclines and exhilarating descents, here and there, the countryside around Malmesbury and North Wiltshire seemed ideal for exploration on two wheels – along quiet country lanes, over rivers and streams, under railway lines. Here you will find ancient landscapes, snapshots of village life, farms, churches and chapels, remote settlements, apparently little changed by the march of time, but with each generation leaving its mark. For both beginners and experts at the handlebars, the landscape stretching south from the Cotswolds escarpment, via Dauntsey Vale and the Avon Valley to the northern outcrops of the Wiltshire Downs offers almost limitless opportunities for healthy, pleasurable recreation – at your own pace off the beaten track.

My cycling experience began on a series of trikes. For my 11th birthday, Mum and Dad bought me a Raleigh Shopper – painted bottle green with tiny wheels, set in thick white tyres – to cycle a return trip of six miles to school, through the alleyways and leafy avenues of semi-detached 1930s houses of suburban Hornchurch. No-one batted an eye, in those innocent days, about children walking or cycling alone to school. While lacking the elegance of some of my friends' bikes, my sturdy Raleigh provided reliable service, and helped me acquire a lifelong enthusiasm for cycling. Since my school days, I've always owned a bike and used it to shop, get to work or just pop out for a relaxing break. I hope readers will enjoy these bike rides. Happy cycling!

Author and her brother David, Hornchurch, Essex c. 1960

About this Guide

Ranging in length from nine to 31 miles, the featured bike rides are designed to appeal to cyclists of varying abilities and experience. The level of challenge increases progressively from first to last, so less experienced bike riders might like to tackle them in the order that they appear. You may wish to try out the shorter ones two or three times before moving onto the longer routes. Each route is given a star-rating to indicate the level of physical challenge presented:

*	Easy
**	Moderate
***	More challenging

How much time should I allow for each ride?

It depends on how fast you go, weather, wind and road conditions. I reckon on an average of about 6mph on my bike rides, but I'm a slowcoach. I suggest you look at the distance, the star-rating and the introductory description of the ride, when calculating how long to allow. Don't forget to add on any stopping time, if you plan to break for refreshments or linger at some of the places of interest mentioned.

Where will these rides take me – do I need to take OS maps too?

The title illustration shows you at a glance the geographical area featured in this book. It extends to more than 300 square miles – from (north to south) Rodmarton (between Tetbury and Cirencester) down to East Tytherton, near Chippenham; and from (east to west) Lydiard Park, on the outskirts of Swindon, to Badminton. Most of the routes will take you around north Wiltshire, but as Malmesbury lies right at the top of the county, some rides will take you over the border into Gloucestershire.

Most of the routes are contained within the area covered by OS Landranger 173: Swindon & Devizes. The Chavenage and Rodmarton routes take you into the adjoining area, covered by OS Landranger 163: Cheltenham & Cirencester. You shouldn't need to take a map with you, but it may add to your enjoyment if you do.

Where do the rides start and finish?

For the sake of simplicity, all 16 bike rides described here start and finish at the Market Cross, at the top of Malmesbury High Street. However, readers can complete each route by starting (and returning to) any town or village featured along it. Join the relevant route at whatever point is most convenient for where you live, or are visiting, and follow the instructions back to your starting point. On each ride, the numbers that precede each bit of route instruction correspond to the numbers on the sketch map.

The circular Wiltshire Cycle Route (WCR) passes through Malmesbury, and many of the bike rides featured in this guide use short sections of the WCR to leave, and return to, Malmesbury – via Foxley and Norton to the west, and Milbourne to the east.

Triangle, Malmesbury - looking east along Abbey Row

View towards Malmesbury from Foxley Road

What can I see and do along these routes?

The route directions highlight places of interest to help you get the most out of your ride and any regular events that you might like to incorporate or return for another time. Pubs and village shops along the way are mentioned too if you want to take a break, otherwise there are plenty of hostelries to choose from in Malmesbury and Tetbury. Observing the changing seasons and colours enriches every ride, so consider trying them out at different times of year (weather permitting!). In Malmesbury, the Abbey and the Abbey House Gardens (www.abbeyhousegardens.co.uk)

are well worth a visit. For information about regular events you might take in along the way – see Highlights of the Year, on page 127.

How should I prepare for a bike ride?

Ensure you check that your bike is in sound working order before using it. Test your brakes, tyres and lights, particularly; and consider taking a pump and a puncture repair kit on your ride. Use of helmets is a matter of personal choice, of course, as it is not a legal requirement. Some kind of reflective clothing and/or strips attached to the bike are strongly advisable, as is a bell and a padlock. If you need to buy cycle equipment and clothing, I suggest you visit C.H. White, 51, High Street, Malmesbury (tel. 01666-822330), one of the best-known and longest-established cycle shops in the West Country.

Use hand signals to indicate your intentions, and acknowledge the courtesies of other road users when they give way or slow down for you.

If you don't know how to ride a bike, or have doubts about your competence, ask an experienced rider to give you some tuition. Consider joining a local cycling club to help you develop the necessary skills, build up your confidence, as well as your fitness. The Cyclists' Touring Club (www.ctc.org.uk) will help you get on the right track.

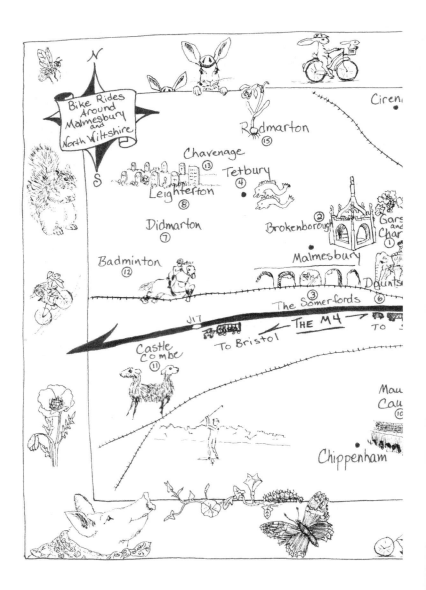

Bike Rides Around Malmesbury and North Wiltshire

N

S

Ciren...

Rodmarton
⑤

Chavenage
⑬

Tetbury
④

Leighterton
⑧

Didmarton
⑦

Brokenboroug...
②

Gars...
and
Char...
①

Malmesbury

Badminton
⑫

Daunts...
⑥

The Somerfords
③

J17

To Bristol

THE M4

TO S...

Castle Combe
⑪

Mau...
Cau...
⑩

Chippenham

Cirencester

Cotswold
Water Park
⑭

Minety
⑤

Garsdon
and
Charlton
①

Callow
Hill
⑨

Dauntsey
⑥

Lydiard
Park
⑯
J16

TO SWINDON

Wootton
Bassett

Maud Heath's
Causeway
⑩

am

The Bike Rides

1. Garsdon & Charlton
2. Brokenborough
3. The Somerfords
4. Tetbury
5. Minety
6. Dauntsey
7. Didmarton
8. Leighterton
9. Callow Hill
10. Maud Heath's Causeway
11. Castle Combe
12. Badminton
13. Chavenage
14. Cotswold Water Park
15. Rodmarton
16. Lydiard Park

mary ray smith

1. GARSDON & CHARLTON

Distance:	9 miles
Pub:	Horse & Groom, Charlton
Map:	OS Landranger 173: Swindon & Devizes
Visiting:	Garsdon, Milbourne & Charlton
Star-rating:	* Easy

Enjoy panoramic views south towards the Wiltshire Downs and the ancient Ridgeway as you pootle along the quiet lanes criss-crossing the countryside east of Malmesbury. Ideal for less experienced cyclists to practise their road skills – and for a quick blast of fresh country air to blow away the cobwebs.

Route:

Facing the High Street from the Market Cross, go left along Oxford Street and left again to take you down Holloway. At the bottom of the hill, just after crossing the river Avon, turn right up Blicks Hill. You may have to get off and push the bike up part of this, as it is quite steep.

1. Cross the main road (A429) with care, as traffic may be travelling fast in both directions, and continue straight ahead through a gate. On reaching a road junction, go right (in effect, it's straight on) through Milbourne.

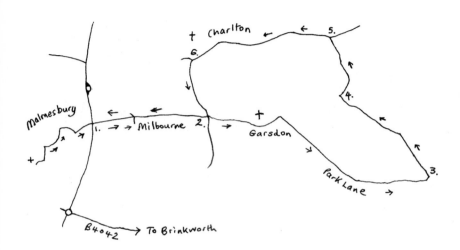

2. After Tanner's Bridge, you soon reach a crossroads. Go straight on towards **Garsdon (A)** soon to pass All Saints Church on your left. At the next junction, turn right in the direction of Brinkworth, along Park Lane and continue for about two miles. Turn left at the T-junction.

Park Lane, east of Garsdon

3. After a few yards you then reach another T-junction. Go left here (signed Charlton) along Pink Lane, and continue for about a mile and a half to the next T-junction.

4. Turn right along Moor Lane, signposted Charlton.

5. At the end of Moor Lane, turn left onto the B4040 towards **Charlton (B)**. Keep going through Charlton past the Horse & Groom (tel. 01666-823904) and the village hall on your right. Stay on the main road as it bends left, soon to leave the village. As you start going downhill, don't go too fast as you need to turn left before reaching the bottom of the hill!

Pub sign, Charlton

6. Take the first turning left, signposted Lea and Garsdon, and continue through Noah's Ark and past the **Bow-in-the-Cloud Vineyard (C)**. Turn right at the next crossroads back towards Milbourne. Once in the village, and as the road bends sharp right, go straight on into a No Through Road soon to pass through a gate and reach a junction with the Malmesbury by-pass (A429). Go straight across the road and follow the lane opposite down Blicks Hill (take care here, it can be gravelly and slippery) to a T-junction. Turn left and follow the one-way system back to the High Street. Turn right onto the High Street soon to arrive at the Market Cross.

Heading west towards Blicks Hill from Milbourne

Notes:

A: **Garsdon:** Originally owned by Malmesbury Abbey, the Manor of Garsdon was given by Henry VIII to his servant Richard Moody after the Dissolution of the Monasteries. While out hawking, Henry fell off his horse into mud, and it was Moody who hauled the rotund monarch back to his feet. Moody's descendant Sir Henry Moody sold the manor to the Washington family of Sulgrave, Northamptonshire. Sir Laurence Washington of Garsdon was the grandson of Laurence Washington of Sulgrave, from whom George Washington (1732-99), the first American president, was descended. A memorial painted with gold stars and red stripes, dedicated to Sir Laurence, was erected on the wall of All Saints Church, Garsdon following his death. The stars and stripes design is thought to have inspired the first American flag sewn a century later.

B: **Charlton Park** lies beyond the turning right – once you are nearly out of the village – towards the church. Built for the first Earl of Suffolk, the Grade I Listed mansion has been described as one of the great country houses of Wiltshire, dating back to 1607. After marrying Lady Elizabeth Howard in 1663, the poet and critic John Dryden lived at Charlton Park from 1665-66. Parts of the mainly Georgian interior have been converted into leasehold apartments. Charlton Park hosted its first four-day World of Music Arts and Dance (WOMAD) in July 2007. The festival had outgrown its previous site at Reading, Berkshire.

C: **Bow-in-the-Cloud Vineyard** was planted in 1992-93 and started producing its award-winning wines in 1995. Visit www.bowinthecloud.co.uk for more information.

2. BROKENBOROUGH

Distance:	11 miles
Pubs:	Rose & Crown, Brokenborough,
	Cat & Custard Pot, Shipton Moyne
Map:	OS Landranger 173: Swindon & Devizes
Visiting:	Brokenborough, Shipton Moyne, Easton
	Grey, Foxley
Star-rating:	* Easy

On the trail of Malmesbury's famous escape artists, the Tamworth Two (pigs), novice and younger cyclists should find this a good route to try out once or twice to get in shape for tackling the longer ones later. From the Fosse Way there are good views south east towards Malmesbury and the Wiltshire Downs.

Route:

At the top of the High Street, facing the Market Cross, turn left along Gloucester Street past the mirror, the Abbey and the Old Bell soon to reach the War Memorial. Cross the road and go up Katifer Lane, to the left of the Three Cups pub.

1. At a T-junction, turn right along West Street, bear left across Horsefair, then turn left along Burnham Road. Follow this as it bends right downhill and go over a

crossroads at the bottom of the hill to join Park Road. On the site of the new houses on your left was

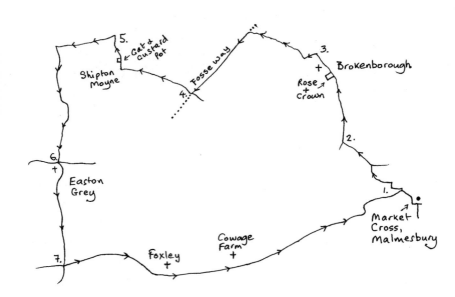

Newman's abattoir, from which the **Tamworth Two (A)** made their great escape.

2. At the end of Park Road, turn right over the river bridge and uphill to Brokenborough. The Rose & Crown (tel. 01666-822302), which has a children's play area and garden, soon appears on your left. Continue in the same direction past Brokenborough church.

Rose & Crown, Brokenborough

3. After passing Church Lane take the next turning left, which begins with a steepish descent. Watch out for potholes and gravel! About a quarter of a mile out of the village, at the top of the hill, turn left onto the **Fosse Way (B)**. Depending on the time of year, and whether the hedges have been trimmed, you may be able to see along here the spires of St Paul's, Malmesbury (left) and St Mary's, Tetbury (right).

4. Just after a farm on your left, turn right off the byway onto a metalled lane towards Shipton Moyne. On reaching the village, ignore the left turn signposted Easton Grey. The Cat & Custard Pot (tel. 01666-880249) is in the centre of the village on your left opposite the village hall. Continue in the same direction through the village.

Polo practice, Shipton Moyne

5. Ignore a drive on the left, then take the next turning left, signposted Westonbirt and Dursley. Take the next left again, opposite a bridleway, towards Easton Grey. Continue past a left turning leading back to Shipton Moyne

6. At the next junction, dog-leg left and right across the B4040 towards Easton Grey. Keep going downhill passing the entrance gates (right) to **Easton Grey House (C)** through the village, over the River Avon (Sherston branch) and then continue uphill.

7. At the next crossroads, take the left turning back towards Malmesbury soon to pass through Foxley. About a quarter of a mile after passing Foxley church look out for a bridleway (left) and track through Cowage Farm which goes past **Bremilham Church (D)**. Continue to the town centre via the Truckle Bridge, Bristol Street, the Triangle War Memorial and Abbey Row.

Bremilham church, Britain's smallest still in service

Notes:

A: **The Tamworth Two**, later nicknamed Butch and Sundance, became international celebrities in January

1998 when they broke out of an abattoir, swam across the Avon and spent nearly two weeks on the run, with television crews and newspaper reporters in hot pursuit. After their re-capture, the pigs were temporarily homed at an animal sanctuary near Chippenham, then bought by the *Daily Mail* and eventually re-settled at a rare breeds farm. For many of us, the sight of huge CNN and BBC lorries, laden with satellite equipment, parked up along Malmesbury High Street, will never be forgotten.

B: The **Fosse Way** runs from Exeter to Lincoln and this section forms part of the county boundary between Wiltshire (left) and Gloucestershire (right). The Romans built this the first arterial road in Britain to link the West Country and the Midlands.

C: **Easton Grey House**, built in the late 18th century, hosted the Duke of Windsor (when still the Prince of Wales) on numerous occasions when he visited the area to hunt with the Duke of Beaufort. Lord Asquith, prime minister from 1908-1916, also stayed at the house for summer holidays. In the 1950s and 1960s, the house accommodated a fashion business Peter Saunders Tweeds, relocated from Scotland to north Wiltshire. The house and gardens were open to the public for many years. Peter Saunders wrote a book *Almost A Fairy Story*, describing the history of the house and his family's connection with it. No known dedication exists for the **Parish Church of Easton Grey** (near the top of the hill). Its rectors from AD 1311-1937 are listed in beautiful script on a wall to the left of the entrance. The tower dates back to the 15th century, although the rest of the church was rebuilt in 1836.

D: **Bremilham Church** is Britain's smallest still in service, measuring just 11ft by 10ft. It was built in the 1800s to replace a larger one on the site, although with Foxley church just up the road, it's not clear why. An annual service is held here on Rogation Sunday.

3. THE SOMERFORDS

Distance: 13½ miles
Refreshments: Rose & Crown, Lea;
Saladin, Little Somerford;
Volunteer Inn, Great Somerford;
Radnor Arms, Corston.
There is a shop at Great Somerford.
Map: OS Landranger 173: Swindon & Devizes
Visiting: Milbourne, Lea, Cleverton, Little and
Great Somerford, Startley, Rodbourne,
Corston
Star-rating: * Easy

A tonic of a ride, with plenty of historical and landscape interest, and refreshment opportunities! Look out for the railway viaduct and water tower at Rodbourne and, on the return leg, the vast expanse of King's Heath, south of Malmesbury.

Route:

With the Market Cross behind you, turn left into Oxford Street, and left again into Holloway. At the bottom of the hill, just after going over the river, turn right up Blicks Hill. Some of you may have to get off and push the bike up part of this, as it is quite steep.

14

1. Cross the main road, and continue straight ahead
    through a gate. On reaching a road junction, go right

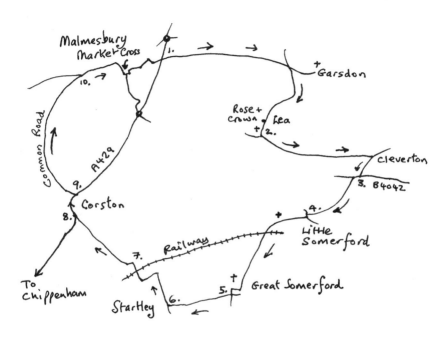

(in effect straight on) through Milbourne. After about
a mile, turn right at a crossroads towards Lea.

2. After passing the Rose & Crown (tel. 01666-824344)
    at Lea, turn left opposite the church into Cresswell
    Lane, which will take you to the hamlet of Cleverton.
    At the next T-junction turn right towards the

Somerfords, passing an attractive little Methodist church on your left.

Cleverton Methodist Church

3. Turn right onto the main road (B4042), and after about 200 yards turn left downhill to Little Somerford. To visit the Saladin (tel. 01666-824222), turn right at the T-junction at the foot of the hill – the pub is then about 100 yards further on, to your left. If not visiting the pub, continue as below.

4. Turn left at the T-junction at the bottom of the hill and almost immediately right towards Great Somerford, soon passing **Little Somerford Church (A)**. Just before going under the railway bridge, note the lane to your left leading to the former Little Somerford railway station, whose platforms still exist. On entering Great Somerford, and just before crossing the river Avon, you pass the former station house, the last house on the right.

Horse and rider, Somerford Show

5.   At the crossroads just before the village shop and the Volunteer Inn (tel. 01249-720316), turn right towards Startley.

6.   As you come into Startley, turn right at a T-junction towards Rodbourne. After crossing the brow of the hill, turn left to Rodbourne Bottom and follow the lane as it bears right and right again to pass under the railway viaduct.

Railway viaduct, Rodbourne Bottom

7. At the T-junction at the top of the hill, turn left towards Corston, passing the water tower. (If you want to see **Rodbourne (B)** church go right at this T-junction and you will soon see the church on your left.) Continue downhill to reach Corston and a T-junction with the A429.

8. Dismount here, turn right and continue along the pavement for about 150 yards, passing the Radnor

Arms (tel. 01666-823389) on the other side of the road. Cross the road when it is safe to do so, remount and continue past Mill Lane on your left.

9.   Take the next left (signposted Foxley) into Common Road. As the road bends gently round to the right, **King's Heath (C)**, also known as Malmesbury Common, can be seen ahead and left.

10.   At the end of Common Road, turn right onto Foxley Road, which takes you back into Malmesbury centre, via Bristol Street, the Triangle War Memorial and Abbey Row, soon to arrive at the Market Cross.

Notes:

A: St John the Baptist Church, Little Somerford contains a memorial to Walter Powell, MP for Malmesbury from 1868 until his mysterious death in 1881. A generous local benefactor and famous balloonist, Powell disappeared without trace while on a research flight in the hot air balloon Saladin in December of that year. The local school is named after him, and the pub takes its the name from the balloon which carried him on his last voyage. The church also has a Royal Coat of Arms (dated 1602) of Queen Elizabeth I, featuring a Tudor dragon in place of the more familiar unicorn.

B: **Holy Rood, Rodbourne:** Of Norman origin, the church has some stained glass by William Morris, Dante Gabriel Rossetti and Ford Maddox Brown. The railway running south of Rodbourne is part of the "cut off" built by the GWR between Wootton Bassett and Patchway north of Bristol, sometimes known as the Badminton line. Opened in 1903, the new line provided more direct rail links from Swindon to the Severn Tunnel and South Wales than the original GWR mainline via Chippenham and Bath to Bristol Temple Meads.

C: **King's Heath:** King Athelstan, grandson of Alfred, and the first King of All England granted a large swathe of land south west of Malmesbury – more than 600 acres – to the burgesses of the town. The gift was made in recognition of the help Malmesbury menfolk gave to King Athelstan in the Battle of Brunanburh in 937 AD when they helped him defeat Anlaf the Dane. The land still belongs to their descendents The Warden and Freemen of Malmesbury, also known as the Old Corporation, which meets as the Court of Athelstan.

4. TETBURY

Distance:	15 miles
Pubs:	Cat & Custard Pot, Shipton Moyne,
	Snooty Fox, Tetbury
Map:	OS Landranger 173: Swindon & Devizes
Visiting:	Shipton Moyne, Westonbirt, Tetbury
Star-rating:	* Easy

Wide open countryside, and quiet country lanes make for a decent short ride. Time it to coincide with the Tetbury Woolsack Races and Street Fair at the end of May on Whit Bank Holiday Monday and you might want to plan an all day excursion. Don't miss Highgrove, the Prince of Wales's emporium in Long Street, described in one newspaper as "the poshest grocery shop in the world". All profits from the enterprise go to the Prince's Charities Foundation.

Route:

Facing the High Street from the Market Cross, go over the pedestrian crossing and turn right past the mirror, and the Old Bell. Bear left by the War Memorial in the direction of Sherston. Once out of town, ignore the first turning right to Brokenborough.

1.   Take the next right to Shipton Moyne. Go straight on through the village – unless you want to stop at the

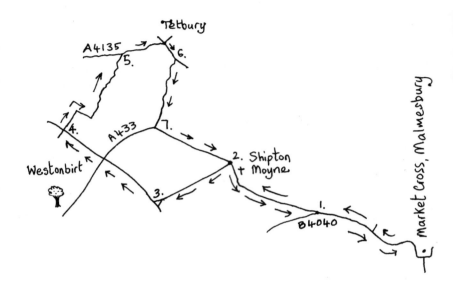

Cat & Custard Pot (tel. 01666-880249) on your left, and keep going in the same direction.

2.   Take the first left beyond the village (about 400 yards after the pub) just past a pair of "Speed limit ends" signs. After about 1¾ miles, take the right fork to meet a T-junction.

3.   Turn right towards Westonbirt and continue for about a mile to the crossroads (junction with the A433) and the Hare & Hounds Hotel. Go straight on (towards Leighterton and Dursley) and continue for about two miles, past the first right turn and the Beaufort Polo Club on your left. Slow down as you approach a dip in the road, and a right turn.

4. Turn right here, signposted Tetbury, and **Hookshouse Pottery** (**A**). Continue along this quiet lane for about 2½ miles, past the turning to Nesley Farm and the pottery (both on the left) to reach a T-junction.

5. Turn right at the T-Junction (A4135 Tetbury-Dursley road) and continue into **Tetbury** (**B**). Turn right at the first crossroads you meet in the town. Continue along Long Street (past the Highgrove shop on your right)

Highgrove shop, Long Street, Tetbury

23

to the mini-roundabout just before the Market House. The Snooty Fox (tel. 01666-502436) is just beyond the mini-roundabout on the left.

Market House, Tetbury

6. Turn right at the mini-roundabout in the direction of Bath, Bristol and Westonbirt (A433). About a mile out of Tetbury look out for a left turn just beyond a plant nursery.

7. Turn left here and continue for about two miles back into Shipton Moyne. Go straight through the village in the direction of Malmesbury and continue to a T-junction with the B4040. Turn left towards

Malmesbury and stay on this road into the town. Turn right by the Triangle War Memorial to pass along Abbey Row soon to reach the Market Cross.

Notes:

A: **Hookshouse Pottery,** established by Christopher White in 1975, uses simple, traditional methods to produce distinctive hand-thrown domestic ware, garden and conservatory pots. For more information visit www.hookshousepottery.co.uk or phone 01666-880297.

B: **Tetbury** hosts its annual Woolsack Races and Street Fair on Whit Bank Holiday Monday. Back in the 17th century, sheep drovers raced each other up and down Gumstool Hill after a few drinks to impress local girls. Happily the modern version is very similar, although women too can compete nowadays. Stuffed with wool, the women's sacks weigh 35 lbs and the men's 60 lbs. The event raises money for local charities.

The brook running along the south eastern edge of Tetbury once separated Wessex from Mercia. It later formed part of the county boundary between Wiltshire and Gloucestershire, although this bit of the border has since been moved to the Fosse Way. The town derives its name from Tette, thought to be the sister of

King Ine of Wessex, who became the Abbess of Wimborne. A pair of dolphins feature on the town's unofficial coat of arms, for reasons unknown, and this distinctive "logo" can be seen around the town on street benches, for example, and in Church Street above the entrance to St Mary's.

Woolsack race, Tetbury

5. MINETY

Distance:	18 miles
Pubs:	Vale of the White Horse Inn, Minety;
	Horse & Groom, Charlton
Map:	OS Landranger 173: Swindon & Devizes
Visiting:	Milbourne, Garsdon, Minety, Charlton
Star-rating:	** Moderate

Wild flower meadows, ancient woodland and rolling farmland off quiet country lanes combine to make this ride a real rural stress-buster. Several stretches have an appealing "middle of nowhere" feel, ideal for quiet contemplation while you pedal away the miles. You pass some glorious nature conservation sites, managed by the Wiltshire Wildlife Trust.

Route:

Looking down the High Street from the Market Cross, turn left into Oxford Street, and left again into Holloway. After crossing the bridge over the Avon, turn right up Blicks Hill. You may have to push the bike up part of this, as it is quite steep. Cross the A429 with care, and continue ahead via a wooden gate along a narrow lane. Go right at the T-junction –

in effect, you go straight on. Continue through Milbourne, and cross over Tanner's Bridge.

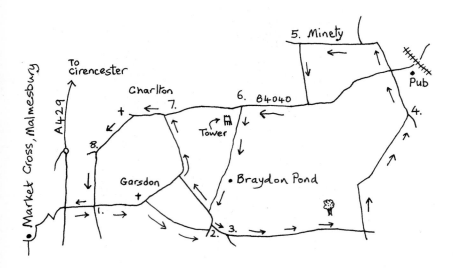

1. At a crossroads, go straight on towards **Garsdon (A)**. Once past the church on your left, turn right at the next junction, signposted Brinkworth and Purton.

2. On reaching a T-junction, turn left, and then next right signposted Purton. Here you are going along the southern edge of Braydon Wood.

3. Take the next turning left, just before a dip in the road. After a couple of miles, you pass alongside the southern boundary of **Ravensroost Wood (B)**. (There is an entrance to the wood just past Grove Farm.)

Looking east towards Garsdon

4. Turn left at the next crossroads towards Minety. Once past Old Ravensroost Farm, look out for an alternative route into Ravensroost Wood (via a bridleway, a few yards past the farm on your left) and shortly afterwards, **Distillery Meadows (C)** and information boards on your left. Continue to a T-junction and turn left soon to reach Minety crossroads. To visit the Vale of the White Horse Inn (tel. 01666-860175), turn right at the crossroads. You will soon see the pub on your right just before the railway bridge. If not visiting the pub go straight ahead at **Minety (D)** crossroads into Silver Street, soon to pass the War Memorial (left) and village school (right).

Vale of the White Horse Inn

Minety Water Tower

5.   After about a mile, you pass Minety Park on your right. Take the next left, a little further on, into Dog Trap Lane. At a T-junction at the end of this road turn right onto the B4040.

6.   After almost a mile, and approaching the brow of a hill, take the turning left to pass the Minety water tower (on your right), visible over many miles around

Malmesbury, and soon Braydon Pond (left). At a T-junction, turn right, and after a mile or so, right again to reach a T-junction with the B4040.

Braydon Pond

7. Turn left towards Charlton, soon to pass the Horse & Groom pub (tel. 01666-823904) on your right. Continue past the village hall and the lane leading to Charlton church to leave the village. Don't go too fast down the hill as you will need to turn left before reaching the bottom of it!

8. Take the first left signposted to Lea and Garsdon, passing the Bow-in-the-Cloud Vineyard at Noah's

Ark on your right. Take the first right to Milbourne, and go over Tanner's Bridge. Once in the village, and where the road bends sharp right, go straight on along a No Through Road. Go through a wooden gate and cross over the A429 with care. Continue along the lane ahead down Blicks Hill (careful here it can be slippery) to reach a T-junction at the bottom of the hill. Turn left and follow the road into Malmesbury Town Centre, passing the short stay car park, to reach a T-junction with the High Street. Turn right to reach the Market Cross at the top of the street.

Notes:

A: **Garsdon:** See notes accompanying Ride 1: Garsdon & Charlton.

B: **Ravensroost Wood** once formed part of the medieval Royal Hunting Forest of Braydon. Now it lies within the Wiltshire Wildlife Trust's largest nature reserve, which includes an important area of semi-natural woodland and hay meadow. Among the species found here are the brown hairstreak butterfly, the small leaved lime, and silver-washed fritillary. Visit www.wiltshirewildlife.org for more information.

C: **Distillery Meadows**: Another Wiltshire Wildlife Trust nature reserve consisting of eight fields. In May, June and early July, they are filled with wildflowers and traditional meadow plant species that have become rare in England. They include sneezewort, saw-wort, devil's bit scabious, yellow rattle and green-winged orchid.

D: The village name **Minety** (originally Myntye or Minty) is thought to derive from the wild mint that once flourished in the area. The main coaching route from Bristol to Oxford used to pass through the southern fringes of Minety (via Malmesbury, Milbourne and Garsdon). The railway line from Swindon to Stroud via Kemble runs to the east and north of the village. The Minety & Ashton Keynes railway station (near what is now the Vale of the White Horse Inn) ran passenger services from 1841 to 1964, and was described by Mike Oakley in his book *Wiltshire Railway Stations* as "an excellent example of the early Brunel 'road-side' or 'chalet' style station". According to the Minety author and historian L.J. Manners, Isambard Kingdom Brunel was often seen on horseback around the village from 1838-41 while surveying the route of the railway for which he was the project engineer.

6. DAUNTSEY

Distance:	18½ miles
Refreshments:	Rose & Crown, Lea;
	Volunteer Inn, Great Somerford;
	Radnor Arms, Corston.
	Village shop at Great Somerford.
Map:	OS Landranger 173: Swindon & Devizes
Visiting:	Milbourne, Lea, Cleverton, Little
	Somerford, Dauntsey, Great Somerford,
	Startley, Rodbourne, Corston
Star-rating:	** Moderate

An extended variation of the Somerfords ride, this route takes you through attractive countryside south west of Malmesbury, past Dauntsey Park and a church with a medieval doom board – designed to put the fear of God into anyone viewing it. Snowdrops and crocuses are especially abundant on the verges around Rodbourne in early spring. You will see (or at least hear) the traffic on the M4 before looping back from Dauntsey towards Malmesbury, but don't let that put you off. Mainly level along quiet country lanes, with some gentle inclines.

Route:

With the Market Cross behind you, turn left into Oxford Street, and left again into Holloway. At the bottom of the hill, just after going over the river, turn

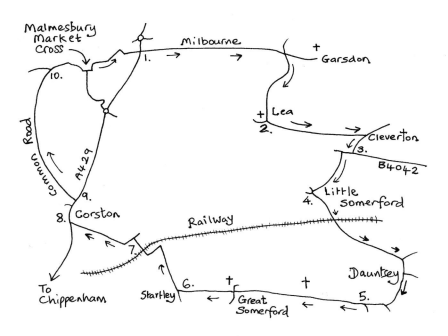

right up Blicks Hill. Some of you may have to get off and push the bike up part of this, as it is quite steep.

1. Cross the main road (A429) and continue straight ahead through a gate. On reaching a road junction, go

right (in effect straight on) through Milbourne. After about a mile, turn right at the crossroads at the top of the hill towards Lea.

2. After passing the Rose & Crown (tel. 01666-824344) at Lea, turn left opposite the church into Cresswell Lane. Keep going for about two miles to the hamlet of Cleverton. Ignore the turning left by Cleverton Farm and continue to a T-junction. Turn right towards the Somerfords, passing the attractive Cleverton Methodist Church on your left.

3. At a T-junction, turn right onto the main road (B4042) and, after about 200 yards, take the first left downhill to Little Somerford.

4. Turn left at the T-junction at Little Somerford and follow the road as it bends left towards Dauntsey and Lyneham. Go under the railway line (Swindon to Bristol Parkway), over Brinkworth Brook and pass an entrance to **Dauntsey Park (A)** on your right. As you approach the village of **Dauntsey (B)**, you may see (or at least hear) the motorway traffic in the distance. Pass the school and old almshouses on your right soon to reach a T-junction.

5. Turn right, signposted Great Somerford. About a mile further on, follow the road as it bends sharp left, taking you past the lane leading to St James the Great

Church (right) and over the River Avon. Once past the Walter Powell primary school (right) note the entrance on your left to the Free Gardens, gifted to the parish of Great Somerford in 1809 after the Rev. Stephen Demainbray arranged the exchange of this field for pieces of common land around the village. At the crossroads in Great Somerford, go straight on towards Startley (unless you wish to stop at the Volunteer Inn (tel. 01249-720316) on your left or the village shop, also on your left opposite the pub). Continue ahead past the converted Manor Farm Stables.

St James the Great, Dauntsey

6. As you come into Startley, turn right towards Rodbourne. After passing over the brow of the hill, take the next left signposted Rodbourne Bottom and follow the lane as it bears slightly uphill and right soon to pass under the splendid railway viaduct.

7. At the T-junction at the top of the hill, turn left towards Corston, passing the water tower – unless you'd like to take a quick detour to see the hamlet of Rodbourne. (If so, turn right here to see **Rodbourne Church (C)**, and the cluster of attractive old houses including the old school, then return to the T-junction and continue downhill to Corston.)

Traditional signpost at Rodbourne   *Pub sign, Corston*

8. On reaching the often busy T-junction (with the A429) at Corston, I recommend that you dismount here, turn right and push your bike along the pavement for about 150 yards, passing the Radnor Arms (tel. 01666-823389) on the other side of the road. Cross the road when it is safe to do so, remount and continue past Mill Lane on your left.

9. Take the next left, signposted Foxley, onto Common Road. Ignore the byway (left) at the brow of a gentle incline and follow Common Road as it bends right gently downhill. **King's Heath (D)**, also known as Malmesbury Common, can be seen stretching ahead and left.

10. At the end of Common Road, turn right onto Foxley Road. Follow the road back towards Malmesbury, over the river and then sharp right up to a T-junction with Bristol Street. Turn right along Bristol Street and on reaching the War Memorial at Triangle, turn right again along Abbey Row, past the Abbey, Birdcage Walk and the mirror. You will soon see the Market Cross, Malmesbury, on your left.

Notes:

A: **Dauntsey Park** was the home of the Danvers family for several generations from 1500 onwards. Henry Danvers, Earl Danby, founded a hospital in

Malmesbury and also a school in the village of Dauntsey. In the late 19th century Sir Henry and Lady Meux acquired Dauntsey Park House. Her ladyship is said to have been a colourful and forthright character – once attending a meeting of the Beaufort Hunt sitting astride an elephant, apparently borrowed from a travelling circus. She also funded an extensive restoration of Wootton Bassett town hall in 1889. The Church of St James the Great, next to Dauntsey Park House, features a newly-restored "doom board", or tympanium, one of only five in England still occupying its original position above the rood screen. Also worth noting are the First World War memorial window and the box pews.

B: The clusters of small settlements that make up the parish of **Dauntsey** were already at some distance from one another before the M4 was built across it. To the south of the parish, Dauntsey Lock, on the route of the Wilts & Berks Canal, was also the location of Dauntsey railway station – on the Wootton Bassett to Chippenham section of Brunel's original Great Western Railway. It opened in 1868, and became the junction station of the Malmesbury branch line in 1877, a role it continued to serve until 1933 when the Dauntsey to Little Somerford section closed.

C: **Rodbourne Church** and **D: King's Heath:** see the notes accompanying Ride 3: The Somerfords.

Common Road and King's Heath

7. DIDMARTON

Distance:	20 miles
Refreshments:	King's Arms, Didmarton;
	Old Royal Ship, Luckington;
	Rattlebone, Sherston.
	There are shops at Luckington and
	Sherston.
Map:	OS Landranger 173: Swindon & Devizes
Visiting:	Sherston, Didmarton, Sopworth,
	Luckington
Star-rating:	** Moderate

A rollicking good ride that takes you through fine countryside and deciduous woodland west of Sopworth. The churches at Didmarton and nearby Oldbury on the Hill are well worth a visit. The King's Arms Inn at Didmarton, roughly half way along the route, welcomes children and also has a good garden. On the return leg you pass through Bullpark Wood, part of the Badminton estate.

Route:

Facing the High Street, with the Market Cross behind you, go over the pedestrian crossing, turn right and go past the mirror. Go left at the War Memorial down

Bristol Street and at the bottom of the hill left again onto Foxley Road.

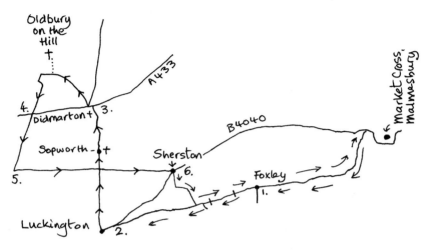

1. Go straight on at Foxley, past the church on your right. After a mile or so continue straight over a crossroads, and another crossroads about two miles further on. On reaching a T-junction, turn right and after about 100 yards take the first left. Go straight on at the next crossroads towards Luckington. Keep going until you have passed alongside a ford at Brook End, using the raised causeway. Cross the road and take the lane uphill opposite you.

2. Turn left at the end onto a main road (B4040) into Luckington. The Old Royal Ship pub (tel. 01666-840222), once owned by the Westonbirt estate, soon

appears on your right. On the left near the pub, on the other side of the main road, stands a classic example of a "tin tabernacle" – Luckington Methodist Church. Turn right after the pub onto the Sopworth road. Go straight on at a crossroads through the village of Sopworth, and continue for about a mile to a T-junction.

St Arild's Church, Oldbury on the Hill

3. Turn left onto the main road (A433), then take the first right signposted Leighterton, then go immediately left towards **Oldbury on the Hill (A)**. St Arild's Church is accessible about half a mile along this narrow lane on the right, off a grass track signposted "Restricted by-way" next to a pond. This track leads to the church entrance. On returning from the church to the lane keep going in the same direction. Turn left at a T-junction to return to the A433. To visit the King's Arms (tel. 01454-238245) turn left and you will see the pub on your left. **St Lawrence's Church (B)** is one of the last buildings on the right at the far (eastern) end of Didmarton.

4. If not visiting the pub or the church, cross the A433 onto the lane opposite, soon to ride through Bullpark Wood on the **Badminton (C)** estate. Depending on the time of year, you may glimpse Worcester Lodge through the trees on your right.

5. Turn left on reaching a T-junction, passing a pair of semi-detached cottages on the corner. Continue straight ahead for about four miles towards Sherston. Go right at the next crossroads into Sherston. The Rattlebone Inn (tel. 01666-840871) soon appears on your right.

6. Take the next turning right opposite the entrance to Holy Cross Church. Continue past Tucks Farm Shop and go down Tanners Hill. At the bottom of the hill, bear left along Bustlers Hill, and start ascending a moderate incline. At the top of the hill follow the road as it bends left. After about a hundred yards take the

Sign, Sherston High Street

Morris dancers, Sherston Boules Festival

left turn signposted Sherston and Malmesbury. Follow
this road over the next two crossroads to pass through
Foxley. Go straight on towards Malmesbury. Once
over the river follow the road to a T-junction. Turn
right onto Bristol Street, then right again by the War
Memorial onto Abbey Row soon to reach the Market
Cross.

Swan and her brood, on the Sherston Avon, Malmesbury

Notes:

A: **Oldbury on the Hill** was a parish in its own right
until 1883 when it merged with Didmarton. St Arild's
Church is thought to have been built in 1150.

According to John Leland, the 16th century writer, St Arild was known as the virgin martyr – killed by the tyrant Mancunius "because she would not consent to lie with him". The only other English church dedicated to St Arild is at Oldbury-on-Severn some 20 miles away.

B: **St Lawrence's Church**, at the eastern end of Didmarton, retains many medieval features and Georgian additions, such as the unusual painted box pews. The plain whitewashed walls are relieved by elegant marble memorials, and lit by a large brass chandelier. A new church St Michael & All Angels was built 300 yards away in 1872, but closed in 1991 after St Lawrence's underwent significant restoration. St Lawrence accompanied St Augustine on his mission to England in 597 and succeeded him as Archbishop of Canterbury in 608.

C: **Badminton:** see the notes accompanying Ride 12: Badminton.

8. LEIGHTERTON

Distance:	20 miles
Refreshments:	Cat & Custard Pot, Shipton Moyne; Jack Hare's Bar, Hare & Hounds, Westonbirt; Royal Oak, Leighterton; Old Royal Ship, Luckington. There is a shop at Luckington.
Map:	OS Landranger 173: Swindon & Devizes
Visiting:	Shipton Moyne, Westonbirt, Didmarton, Sopworth, Luckington, Brook End, Foxley
Star-rating:	** Moderate

This glorious route takes you west of Malmesbury, past the Beaufort Polo Club and north of Westonbirt Arboretum, to Leighterton and its fascinating cemetery. The return leg provides an optional extension to Oldbury on the Hill and Didmarton.

Route:

Facing the High Street from the Market Cross, go over the pedestrian crossing, right past the mirror, and the Old Bell, and bear left by the War Memorial in the direction of Sherston. Once out of town, ignore the first turning right to Brokenborough.

1. Take the next right to Shipton Moyne. Go straight on through the village, passing the Cat & Custard Pot

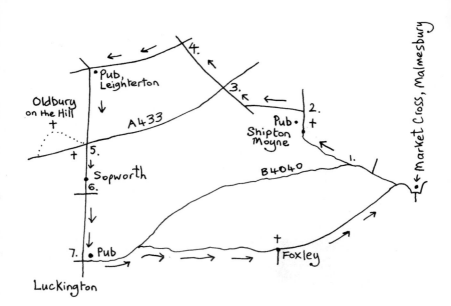

(tel. 01666-880249) on your left, and keep going in the same direction.

2. Take the first left beyond the village (about 400 yards after the pub) just past a pair of "Speed limit ends" signs. After about 1¾ miles, take the right fork to

meet a T-junction. Turn right towards Westonbirt and continue for about a mile to the crossroads (junction with the A433) and the Hare and Hounds Hotel (tel. 01666-880233).

3. Go straight on (towards Leighterton and Dursley) and continue for about two miles, past the first right turn and the **Beaufort Polo Club (A)** on your left. Slow down as you approach a dip in the road, near a crossroads.

Lane between Westonbirt and Leighterton

4. Turn left, signposted Leighterton. After two miles or so, and a bend in the lane, you will see **Leighterton Cemetery (B)** on your right. At the next crossroads, turn left past The Royal Oak (tel. 01666-890250) in the direction of Knockdown and Didmarton. Go straight on towards Didmarton at the next crossroads near a fine duck pond.

Leighterton Cemetery

5.   Just before a T-junction with the A433, you can take an optional two mile extension (right) to see St Arild's Church, at Oldbury on the Hill along a narrow lane. **Optional extension:** Go along the lane and pull up at a "Restricted By-Way" sign. Walk up a grassy track on your right to reach the church entrance about 200 yards up the hill. Return and then continue along the lane past farm buildings to reach a T-junction. Go left, soon to meet the A433, and left again onto the

main road through Didmarton past the King's Arms (tel. 01454-238245) on your left and St Lawrence's Church (right) on your way out of the village. Take the first right signposted Sopworth. If not taking the optional extension, turn left onto the A433, and take the next right to Sopworth.

6. Continue through Sopworth and go straight on towards Luckington.

Foxley Church

7. Just before the first crossroads in **Luckington (C)** turn left past the Old Royal Ship (tel. 01666-840222) and join the B4040 in the direction of Malmesbury.

After passing the cemetery, take the next right to Brook End. Go straight on past a ford (use the raised causeway – the water can be too deep to cycle through safely) and then continue across the next two crossroads. Go right at the next T-junction and left at the next junction. Keep going in the same direction through Foxley towards Malmesbury, via Foxley Road, Bristol Street and Abbey Row soon to reach the Market Cross.

Notes:

A: **Beaufort Polo Club** is run by Simon and Claire Tomlinson, whose son Luke was among the campaigners who invaded the chamber of the House of Commons in September 2004 in protest at the Government Bill banning fox-hunting. The Princes William and Harry have played regularly at the club in recent years. The Duke of Beaufort is the club's president. Club events raise thousands of pounds for charities. Weekend matches and tournaments are held from May to September.

B: **Leighterton Cemetery:** Foreseeing the vital role of aircraft in warfare, the British Government decided in 1911 that the Dominions – Australia, New Zealand and Canada – should have their own Royal Air Forces. Only Australia formed one. Trainee pilots flew from airfields at Leighterton and

Minchinhampton, and some died young in accidents at the controls of their Sopwith Camels. The cemetery contains the graves of 24 Australian airmen, who died between 1918-1930. The Prince of Wales unveiled a stone memorial to them here in 1994.

C: **Luckington:** The late John Thaw, who played Inspector Morse in the popular TV series, and his wife Sheila Hancock had a home in the village for many years. Both Luckington Court and the Church of St Mary and St Ethelbert featured in Andrew Davies' celebrated BBC TV adaptation of *Pride and Prejudice*. Churchill's "Spymaster" Major-General Sir Stewart Menzies (1890-1968), head of the Secret Intelligence Service during World War II lived at Bridges Court, Luckington for most of his life. Sir Stewart was the stepson of Sir George Holford of Westonbirt, a keen horseman and Beaufort Hunt member. Known as "C" to his colleagues, Sir Stewart is said to have inspired the fictional intelligence chief "M" in Ian Fleming's James Bond spy thrillers.

9. CALLOW HILL

Distance:	29 miles
Refreshments:	Volunteer Inn, Great Somerford;
	New Inn, Upper Seagry;
	Star Inn, Hullavington;
	Vine Tree, Norton.
	There are shops at Great Somerford and Hullavington.
Map:	OS Landranger 173: Swindon & Devizes;
Visiting:	Milbourne, Garsdon, Braydon, Somerford Common, Callow Hill, Grittenham, Dauntsey, Great Somerford, Upper Seagry, Lower Stanton, Stanton St Quinton, Hullavington, Norton, Foxley
Star-rating:	** Moderate

The panoramic views west from Callow Hill towards the Bristol Channel and Welsh hills, followed by an exhilarating descent into Dauntsey Vale, provide a treat of a ride. Mainly level with a few modest inclines along quiet lanes through open countryside and some woodland. Maybe take refreshments with you as the pubs are located along the second half of the route.

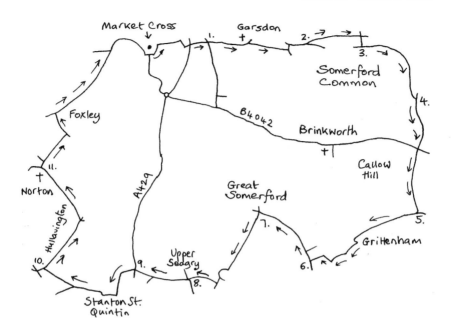

Route:

Looking down the High Street from the Market Cross, turn left into Oxford Street, and left again into Holloway. After crossing the bridge over the Avon, turn right up Blicks Hill. You may have to push the bike up part of this, as it is quite steep. Cross the A429 with care, and continue ahead through a wooden gate onto a narrow lane. Go right at the T-junction (in effect, straight on). Continue through Milbourne, and cross over Tanner's Bridge.

1. At a crossroads, go straight on towards Garsdon. Once past the church on your left, turn right at the next junction signposted Brinkworth and Purton. On reaching a T-junction, turn left, and then almost straight away turn right – signposted Purton. Here you are going along the southern edge of Braydon Wood. Carry on for about half a mile with trees on each side of the road.

2. Take the next left turning just before a dip in the road, so that you have the woodland on your left and, on your right a field, beyond a hedge. Keep going for about three miles to reach a crossroads. Turn right here, signposted Brinkworth to go gently uphill soon to reach a T-junction on the northern edge of **Somerford Common (A)**.

3. Turn left at this junction, noting the charming Braydon Methodist Church (left) about 100 yards further on. As you go over the brow of the hill there are lovely views beyond the hedge line on your left. Soon you reach a T-junction with Wood Lane.

4. Turn right towards Callow Hill, along a section of the Wiltshire Cycleway, and after about a mile you reach a crossroads with B4042 Malmesbury to Swindon road. Cross the road with care and continue straight ahead, signposted Grittenham and Tockenham along

Dauntsey Vale – the view west from Callow Hill

Callow Hill (B). Soon a wonderful panoramic view opens up on your right towards Dauntsey Vale and beyond. Continue downhill over the railway line and shortly under the M4. On the skyline to your left is Wootton Bassett, and the tower of St Bartholomew's Church.

5. When you reach a T-junction, turn right, signposted Dauntsey and Chippenham. Stay on this road for about 3 miles, passing through **Grittenham (C)**. Ignore a turning left (Trow Lane) and after half a mile follow the same road (Sodom Lane) as it bends right

in the direction of the motorway soon to reach another T-junction.

6.   Turn right, signposted Great Somerford and Brinkworth, and follow the road over the M4. Go straight on in the direction of Great Somerford, ignoring the turning (right), signposted Malmesbury and Brinkworth.

Lane under the M4 south of Callow Hill

7.   On reaching the crossroads at Great Somerford, turn left past the Volunteer Inn (tel. 01249-720316) and the village shop and continue towards Seagry. Continue past a sign (left) for Lower Seagry and the church, but take the next right signposted Upper

Seagry and Stanton, soon to fork right on approaching a crossroads.

Pub sign, Great Somerford

8. Cross the road and go straight on past the New Inn (tel. 01249-721083) at Upper Seagry and soon a former Primitive Methodist Chapel (both on your left). Go down the hill out of the village and soon up a modest incline, passing woods on each side and undulating countryside. After emerging from the woods, take the next turning right to Lower Stanton. Stay on this road over a brook and through the village to meet a T-junction with the A429 Chippenham-Cirencester road.

9. Turn left and almost immediately right, signposted Buckley Barracks (alternatively dismount at the T-junction and use the pedestrian crossing on your right). Continue past the barracks (right), go downhill and up a modest hill. You will soon see one of the old turf-covered hangars (right) of the former RAF Hullavington. At the next T-junction, turn right signposted Hullavington and Grittleton soon to pass through Stanton St Quintin and return to open countryside. Ignore the sign (left of the venison farm) to Castle Combe, and follow the road as it bends right, signposted Hullavington.

10. At a T-junction, turn right and go through Hullavington, passing the Star Inn (tel. 01666-837535) and church on your left and a shop and garage on your right. At the next crossroads, turn left signposted Norton and Sherston. Pass under the railway line and, just after it, the former station master's house on the right. Continue for about a mile and a half.

11. After crossing a bridge on your approach to Norton, take the next right, signposted Foxley and Malmesbury. Stay on this road as it crosses a ford and pass the Vine Tree (tel. 01666-837654) on your left. On reaching a T-junction at Foxley, turn right to return to Malmesbury. Keep going on this road to return to the town centre and Market Cross via Bristol Street and Abbey Row.

Notes:

A: **Somerford Common** was part of the ancient forest of Braydon which once covered much of north Wiltshire, providing venison for the Royal Court and firewood, charcoal and building materials for local people. Extending to 200 acres, Somerford Common was acquired by the Forestry Commission and

Log pile, Somerford Common

replanted in the 1960s, although some areas of semi-natural growth, particularly ash and oak, were retained. The Common is an important site for woodland butterflies and moths.

B: **Callow Hill** was on the route of the annual Brinkworth Cycle Race in the 1950s and 1960s. Competitors started and finished at the village cycle shop, going via School Hill, Grittenham, Lyneham, then back up Callow Hill. The winner received the Mark Chesterman Memorial Cup, honouring the founder of the cycle shop. Callow Hill later became the focus of a high profile campaign against proposals for a waste tip on more than 80 acres of farmland. The Friends of Dauntsey Vale organised a series of community walks on the footpaths crossing the land under threat. The planning application was subsequently withdrawn.

C: **Grittenham** consists largely of farms and cottages, strung out along Dauntsey Vale, south of Brinkworth, and is well known to animal lovers for its long-established animal sanctuary at Old Farm, just by the sharp bend left in the road as you leave the village.

10. MAUD HEATH'S CAUSEWAY

Distance: 24 miles
Refreshments: Radnor Arms, Corston;
                   New Inn, Upper Seagry;
                   Bell House Hotel & Vintage Inn, Sutton
                   Benger;
                   Foxham Inn, Volunteer Inn, Great
                   Somerford.
                   There are shops at Great Somerford and
                   Christian Malford
Map: OS Landranger 173: Swindon & Devizes
Visiting: Corston, Rodbourne, Sutton Benger, East
                   Tytherton, Foxham, Christian Malford,
                   The Somerfords, Lea
Star-rating: ** Moderate

*On this exhilarating ride you go over the M4, under the
Swindon to Cardiff railway, over the River Avon and pass
alongside a medieval causeway through Dauntsey Vale –
pancake flat open countryside beneath hills rising to the
south towards Lyneham and Calne. Some lanes can flood
in places after heavy, prolonged rain, so you may want to
save this one for a warm dry spell.*

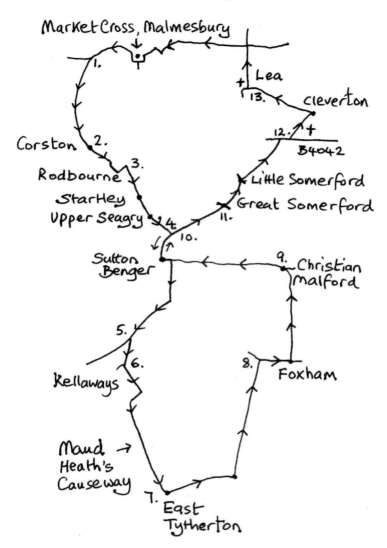

Market Cross, Malmesbury

1.

Lea

13.

Cleverton

12.

B4042

Corston   2.

3.

Rodbourne

Little Somerford

Starley

Great Somerford

Upper Seagry   4   11.

10.

Sutton Benger   9. Christian Malford

5.

Kellaways   6.

8.   Foxham

Maud →
Heath's
Causeway

7.

East Tytherton

Route:

From the Market Cross, Malmesbury, facing the High Street, go over the pedestrian crossing and turn right past the mirror, the Abbey and the Old Bell. At the T-junction in front of the War Memorial, turn left along Bristol Street. Where the road bends right at the foot of a hill, turn left into Foxley Road and cross the river Avon (Sherston branch).

1. Take the first turning left into Common Road. After about a mile **King's Heath (A)** appears on your right. On approaching Corston, and just after a 30mph sign, look out for three bungalows on your right. After the third bungalow, detour right along a bridleway if you wish to visit the **Corston Quarry and Pond (B)** nature reserve. Otherwise continue to a T-junction with the A429.

2. Turn right through Corston. Just after the Radnor Arms (tel. 01666-823389) on your right and the bus stop (left), take the first left signposted Rodbourne. As you begin to ascend the hill, you should see Rodbourne water tower over to your left. Keep going past the church. After passing out of the village you soon reach a T-junction.

3. Turn right, signposted Startley and Upper Seagry, downhill soon to pass under the railway line

(Swindon to Cardiff). Keep going uphill, and pass through Startley. At Upper Seagry, pass the New Inn (tel. 01249-721083) on the right, and continue straight ahead towards Sutton Benger.

4. At a T-junction turn right towards Sutton Benger and Chippenham. Go over the motorway. Look out for the **Vintage Inn (C)** (tel. 01249-720247), and La Flambé restaurant, on your left just as you come into Sutton Benger and reach a T-junction. Opposite you is the Bell House Hotel (tel. 01249-720401). Turn left at the T-junction, and take the first right (Sutton Lane) towards East Tytherton.

5. After about two miles, take a left turning, signposted East Tytherton and Calne, soon to pass under the Swindon-Chippenham railway line. At a T-junction you see **Maud Heath's Causeway (D)** straight ahead of you.

6. Turn left over the River Avon to ride alongside the causeway, soon passing the tiny St Giles Church, Kellaways, on your right.

7. On reaching East Tytherton follow the road round to the left and go straight on, past the fine Moravian Church (left), in the direction of Foxham and back out into open countryside. After about a mile, take a left turning towards Foxham.

M4 viewed from the bridge, near Sutton Benger

Maud Heath's Causeway, by the Avon at Kellaways

8. After a sign indicating you are coming into Foxham, turn right, signposted Foxham and Hilmarton. Take the next left to pass the Foxham Inn (tel. 01249-740665), and the next left to pass under the railway again. Go right at a T-junction through Christian Malford, passing the village shop on your left.

Lane between Foxham and Christian Malford

9. On meeting a main road (B4069), turn left, signposted Chippenham, cross the river Avon again, and return to

Sutton Benger. Take the first right out of the village just past the church, signposted Seagry and Great Somerford, and cross over the M4.

10. Go straight on past the turning (left) to Seagry and continue ahead in the direction of Great Somerford.

11. Go straight over the Great Somerford crossroads. The Volunteer Inn (tel. 01249-720316) is on your left here, and the village shop on your right. Go over the river Avon, and under the railway (again) into Little Somerford. At a T-junction, go left and almost immediately right uphill.

12. At the next T-junction turn right onto the B4042, and shortly first left, signposted Cleverton, past the Methodist Church (right) to a junction with a fine traditional signpost. Turn left here towards Lea.

13. On reaching the next T-junction, turn right past Lea church and the Rose & Crown (tel. 01666-824344) and keep going past the primary school. At the next crossroads, turn left towards Milbourne. Once in the village, and as the road bends right, go straight on into a No Through Road and through a gate at the end of it to reach a junction with the Malmesbury by-pass (A429). Cross the road with care and go straight on along the lane opposite you downhill to a T-junction. Turn left and follow the one-way system back to a junction with Malmesbury High Street. Turn right for the Market Cross.

Notes:

A: **Kings Heath:** See the notes accompanying Ride 3: The Somerfords.

B: **Corston Pond**, an important habitat for toads, was created in the 1950s out of the deepest part of an old limestone quay. The summer wildflowers that encircle the pond include scabious, oxeye daisies and orchids. The nature reserve, owned by Malmesbury St Paul Without Parish Council is looked after by villagers.

C: The **Vintage Inn** is said to have been the birthplace of Quaker and chocolate manufacturer Joseph Fry (1728-1787) who spent many years investigating the therapeutic properties of chocolate before going on to exploit its commercial potential as confectionery. His business became J.S. Fry & Sons, and was merged with Cadbury's in 1919. Plans to close the Cadbury's factory at Keynsham near Bristol were announced in 2007.

D: **Maud Heath's Causeway** dates back to 1474. A wealthy widow, Maud Heath of East Tytherton, donated land and property for the building of the causeway, so that people could transport their animals and farm produce across the flood plain to Chippenham market "dry shod". It runs for four and a half miles from the top of Wick's Hill to Chippenham Clift. A monument dedicated to her memory was erected in 1698 beside the river at Kellaways. In 1838, the Marquess of Lansdowne and William Bowles financed the construction of a second memorial at Wick's Hill, depicting a seated Maud Heath on top of a high stone column staring out towards Kellaways. The inscription reads:

Thou who dost pause on this aerial hight (sic)
Where Maud Heath's Pathway winds in shade or light
Christian Wayfarer in a world of strife
Be still and ponder on the path of life

11. CASTLE COMBE

Distance:	23 miles
Refreshments:	Vine Tree, Norton;
	Neeld Arms, Grittleton;
	Castle Inn, Castle Combe;
	Star Inn, Hullavington.
	There is a village shop at Hullavington.
Map:	OS Landranger 173: Swindon & Devizes
Visiting:	Foxley, Norton, Grittleton, Castle Combe,
	Sevington, Leigh Delamere, Hullavington
Star-rating:	*** More challenging

Contrast the picturesque charms of Castle Combe with some of the quirkier and less known architectural gems on a ride that takes you over and alongside the M4. As you'll discover, there's more to Leigh Delamere than a motorway services area and a branch of M&S. Don't miss the old school at Sevington which recreates a typical Victorian school day for visiting children. Mainly level, with a few inclines.

Route:

From the Market Cross, Malmesbury go over the pedestrian crossing, turn right past the mirror and the

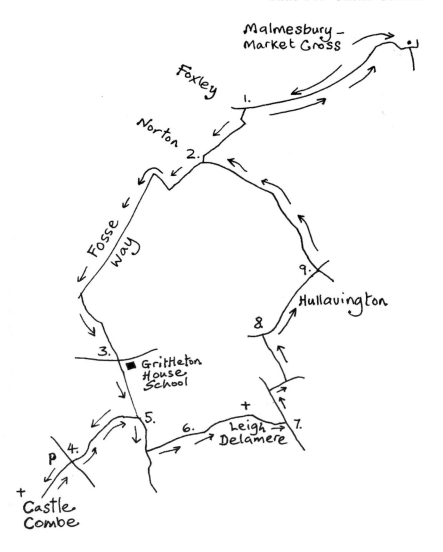

Malmesbury –
Market Cross

Foxley

1.

Norton

2.

Fosse Way

9.

Hullavington

8.

3.

Grittleton
House
School

5.

6.

Leigh
Delamere

7.

P

4.

+
Castle
Combe

75

Old Bell. At the War Memorial, turn left into Bristol Street and, by the dip in the road, next left into Foxley Road. After crossing over the river, ignore the next turning left (Common Road) and continue straight ahead into Foxley.

1. After passing Foxley church (on your right), turn left towards Norton, passing alongside the longer side of the green. On reaching Norton, you will see the Vine Tree (tel. 01666-837654) on your right. Continue in the same direction. Bear left at the ford (ignoring the right turn there) up to a T-junction.

2. At a T-junction, turn right signposted Sherston, and pass Norton Manor on your right. Ignore the turning on the left to Farleaze, but take the next left by a red post box. You are now on a tarmac section of the Fosse Way, open to motor traffic. Continue on it for about three miles towards Grittleton. Go over the Swindon to Cardiff railway and straight on at the next crossroads. Ignore a No Through Road on the right.

3. At the crossroads in Grittleton, go straight on past the entrance to **Grittleton House School (A)** along the road to Chippenham and Yatton Keynell. (You can detour left at the crossroads to visit the Neeld Arms (tel. 01249-782470), just the other side of Grittleton church on the left.) Go over the M4, and take the first turning right to Castle Combe. Note the unusual bell turret of West Foscote House on your right.

4. After about a mile and a quarter, you reach a T-junction. Turn left here and almost immediately right towards **Castle Combe (B)** passing the visitors' car park on your right. Continue downhill (watch out for pedestrians walking in the road and parked cars on the left) to enter the village via the Market Cross and the old mounting block to the left of it. The Castle Inn is on your right. Return up the hill and go back towards

View south from the bridge, Castle Combe

Grittleton the way you came – left at the T-junction near the car park, then first right signposted Grittleton.

5. At the T-junction near the motorway, turn right towards Chippenham and Yatton Keynell. After a road sign indicating a crossroads ahead, take the next left towards Sevington and Leigh Delamere. At Sevington you will see the **Victorian School (C)** on your left.

St Margaret's Church, Leigh Delamere

6. Continue straight ahead for about a mile, over the motorway to reach the hamlet of **Leigh Delamere**

(**D**). Go straight on through Leigh Delamere, past the church on your left and the woods on your right to reach a T-junction.

7. Turn left and pass a property on the right called The Chase. Take the next right signposted to Hullavington, and follow the road as it bends left past a junction with a minor lane on the right.

8. At a T-junction, opposite a No Through Road to Surrendell, turn right towards Hullavington. On passing through the village, you will see the Star Inn (tel. 01666-837535) on your left, and a garage and a village shop on the right. Keep going soon to pass the primary school on your left. After passing the cemetery you soon reach a T-junction.

9. Turn left towards Norton and go under the railway. Pass the old station master's house on your right and as you climb the hill, watch out for **Bradfield Manor (E)** on the left. Keep going for about 1.5 miles. After passing West Lodge and going over a little bridge you soon pass a turning left to Norton church. Take the next right, signposted Foxley and Malmesbury. Stay on this road as it crosses a ford and pass the Vine Tree (tel. 01666-837654) again. On reaching Foxley, turn right at the T-junction towards Malmesbury, and keep going until you cross the river and reach a T-junction with Bristol Street. Turn right here and go right again at the Triangle War Memorial to pass along Abbey Row, soon to reach the Market Cross.

Notes:

A: **Grittleton House** was built for Joseph Neeld, who in 1828 inherited nearly a £1 million at the age of 39 from his great-uncle the silversmith Phillip Rundell. Neeld became MP for Chippenham two years later and built the attractive houses at Grittleton and nearby Alderton. His disastrous marriage to Lady Caroline Ashley-Cooper, daughter of Lord Shaftesbury, ended in the law courts, and the house was only completed after Neeld's death in 1856. After the ownership of the property passed to the Shipp family in 1973, an independent school was established at the house.

B: **Castle Combe** was transformed into a fictional fishing port for the filming of *Dr Dolittle* (1967), and voted the most beautiful village in England a year later. The Manor House, which dates back to the 14th century, is now a hotel, with a much-admired golf course. The Castle Combe motor racing circuit, formerly a World War II airfield, lies about a mile north east of the village.

C: **Sevington Victorian School** was built in 1848 by James Thompson for Joseph Neeld of Grittleton as the latter bought up neighbouring farms and villages to extend his considerable estate. Its unusual bell turret was originally part of St Margaret's Church, Leigh Delamere. Miss Elizabeth Squire was the schoolmistress for 50 years until 1913. Run by an educational trust since 1991, the school now offers children from all over the West Country the chance to recreate a typical Victorian school day, and play with reproduction toys such as hobby horses and hoops.

D: **Leigh Delamere** is best known for its motorway services, opened in 1972, and now run by Moto. Part of the complex serving east-bound M4 traffic can be glimpsed through trees on your right as you pass out of the village. The bell turret on St Margaret's church is a copy of the original, now on top of Sevington school, according to Pevsner. The original church was demolished and re-built by Joseph Neeld of Grittleton who also funded the construction of the parsonage and almshouses to the east of the church.

E: **Bradfield Manor:** see the notes accompanying Ride 12: Badminton.

12. BADMINTON

Distance:	25 miles
Refreshments:	Vine Tree, Norton;
	Neeld Arms, Grittleton;
	Star, Hullavington;
	Fox & Hounds, Acton Turville.
	There are shops at Hullavington and
	Acton Turville.
Map:	OS Landranger 173: Swindon & Devizes
Visiting:	Foxley, Norton, Hullavington, Grittleton,
	Littleton Drew, Acton Turville,
	Badminton, Alderton.
Star-rating:	*** More challenging

Explore the lanes and villages around "Beaufortshire", the rolling acres owned by the Duke of Beaufort – one of England's largest privately-owned estates. Don't miss the magnificent duck pond at Alderton and the attractive covered well at Acton Turville.

Route:

From the Market Cross, Malmesbury go over the pedestrian crossing, turn right past the mirror and the Old Bell. At the War Memorial, turn left into Bristol

Street and, by the dip in the road, next left into Foxley
Road.

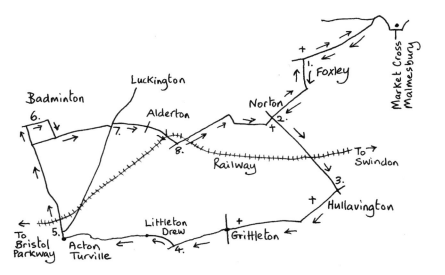

1. At Foxley turn left to Norton, passing alongside the
length of the green. On reaching Norton, you will see
the Vine Tree (tel. 01666-837654) on your right.
Continue in the same direction.

2. At a T-junction, turn left towards Hullavington. (To
see **Norton Church (A),** take the turning almost
immediately right.) Just before a railway bridge and
the former station master's house on the left, look out
for **Bradfield Manor (B)** on your right.

3.   At the next crossroads, turn right towards Hullavington and go straight through the village past the Star Inn (tel. 01666-837535). On emerging into countryside, you will see between gaps in the hedge on your left a couple of the old aircraft hangars built on the former **RAF Hullavington (C)** air base. On reaching Grittleton, continue straight ahead past the Neeld Arms (tel. 01249-782470) towards Littleton Drew.

Canopied well, Acton Turville

4.   Take the next right, just before the motorway, where you see the village entrance sign for Littleton Drew, and at a T-junction on the edge of the village, right again through Littleton Drew. Ignore the Alderton Road on your right and continue on the road as it bends left.

5. On reaching a T-junction at Acton Turville, note the old canopied well, in front of you, originally the site of a sanctuary dating back to Saxon times. From here

Former toll house, Acton Turville

the Fox & Hounds (tel. 01454-218224), to your left, is visible. (An attractive former toll house stands

85

opposite the pub.) Turn right at this junction towards **Badminton (D)**. As you head north out of the village, look out for a No Through Road on your right, at the end of which you can glimpse the former Badminton railway station site. Continue into Badminton, keeping the green and cricket ground on your right.

6. Turn right at a T-junction, and right again past the Memorial Hall. At the end of this road, turn left in the direction of Luckington to pass Badminton Park on your left. A little later, follow the road right, signposted Sherston and Malmesbury.

Beaufort Arms, High Street, Badminton

7. At a T-junction, turn left and then almost immediately right towards Alderton whose splendid pond (on your left), given to the village in 1970 by the Neeld family, is home to more than 20 species of ducks. At a T-junction, go right and then the next left soon to cross over a railway line (Swindon to Bristol Parkway).

Ducks, Alderton Pond

8. Here you are on part of the ancient Fosse Way. After passing a turning to Farleaze, take the next right to Norton. On entering the village, watch out for **Norton Manor (E)** on your left, and a large walled garden opposite. Go left at the next junction and keep going

Pub sign, Norton

past the Vine Tree all the way to the T-junction at Foxley. Turn right for Malmesbury and after crossing the river on the outskirts of town, turn right into Bristol Street. At the War Memorial, turn right along Abbey Row soon to reach the Market Cross.

Notes:

A: **All Saints, Norton:** "Humble with a presumptuous bell-turret" was Pevsner's verdict on this church, in a beautiful and tranquil spot, next to the walled garden opposite Norton Manor.

B: **Bradfield Manor** is one of the few surviving great halls of the 15th century. According to the antiquarian writer John Aubrey, Bradfield was once a distinct medieval parish with its own chapel. William Collingbourne, its owner of the manor in the late 15th century was executed in 1485 for conspiring against Richard III and plotting to have Henry Tudor, the Earl of Richmond, installed on the Throne in his place. In November 2004, ex-Tory MP and junior minister Neil Hamilton and his wife Christine bought Bradfield Manor for a reported £1 million.

C: **RAF Hullavington** began operating in 1937, and later expanded to include an Aircraft Storage Unit, one of nine operating around the country at the outbreak of World War II. After an MoD review in the early 1990s, the RAF moved out, and before long the army moved in (9 Supply Regiment Royal Logistics Corps). Its history is chronicled in David Berryman's book *Wiltshire Airfields in the Second World War.*

D: **Badminton** has been the home of the Somerset family since 1608 when the Manor was purchased by Edward Somerset 4th Earl of Worcester. Since 1682 the family, descended from Edward III, has been headed by the Duke of Beaufort whose motto *Mutare vel timere sperno* means "I scorn to change or to fear". The present mansion combines 17th and 18th century construction in the Palladian style. The 10th Duke of Beaufort was Master of the Horse (1936-78) to three monarchs – Edward VIII, George VI and Elizabeth II – and he started the world-famous Badminton Horse Trials, which are held in early May. On a rainy day in the mid-19th century, the game of badminton was invented by the great aunts of the 10th Duke in the Front Hall, whose dimensions were subsequently adopted to mark out the early badminton courts. James Lees-Milne, the architectural historian and prolific diarist (1908-1997), lived at Badminton in later life.

E: **Norton Manor** was reputedly owned by Malmesbury Abbey until the Reformation. In 1547, it was granted to Sir John Bridges, later Lord Chandos of Sudeley in recognition of his service to Henry VIII. One owner, the fourth Lord Holland, described it as King Athelstan's hunting lodge. Much of the Manor's land and properties were held by the Estcourt family of Shipton Moyne in the 16th and 17th centuries.

13. CHAVENAGE

Distance: 25 miles

Refreshments: Cat & Custard Pot, Shipton Moyne; Hare & Hounds, Westonbirt

Maps: OS Landranger 173: Swindon & Devizes; and 163 Cheltenham & Cirencester

Visiting: Shipton Moyne, Tetbury, Chavenage, Long Newnton, Charlton

Star-rating: *** More challenging

A longer version of the Tetbury route, this one takes you past the beautiful Elizabethan manor house at Chavenage, which opens to the public on certain days. You might want to incorporate a visit to Chavenage House to add interest to a ride that promises miles of freewheeling fun on near empty country lanes.

Route:

Facing the High Street from the Market Cross, go over the pedestrian crossing and turn right into Gloucester Street past the mirror and the Old Bell Hotel. Bear left by the War Memorial in the direction of Sherston. Once out of Malmesbury, ignore the first turning right to Brokenborough.

1. Take the next right to Shipton Moyne. Go straight on through the village, passing the Cat & Custard Pot

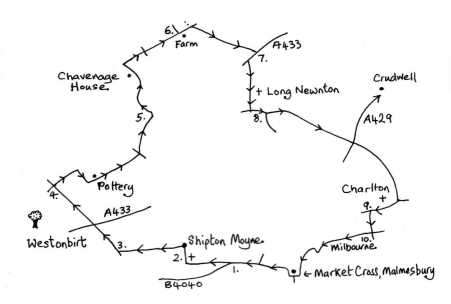

(tel. 01666-880249) on your left, and keep going in the same direction.

2. Take the first left beyond the village (about 400 yards after the pub) just past a pair of "Speed limit ends" signs, in the direction of Westonbirt. After about 1¾ miles, keep right to join the road leading to Westonbirt.

3. Turn right towards Westonbirt and continue for about a mile to the crossroads (junction with the A433) and the Hare & Hounds Hotel (tel. 01666-880233). Go straight on (towards Leighterton and Dursley) and continue for about two miles, past the first right turn and the Beaufort Polo Club on your left. Slow down as you approach a dip in the road, and a crossroads.

Hotel sign, Westonbirt

4. Turn right at the crossroads, signposted **Tetbury** and **Hookshouse Pottery** (**A**). Continue along this quiet lane for about 2½ miles, past the turning to Nesley Farm and the pottery (both on the left) to reach a crossroads. Cross the road (A4135) and continue straight ahead along the lane opposite, signposted Chavenage. At the top of the incline, there are far reaching views (right) towards Tetbury church and beyond. On a clear day you may see Cherhill Down near Calne and some of the clumps of beech trees on the Ridgeway. Watch out for a steep descent to the next junction.

5. Turn left at the bottom of the hill. After about half a mile you will see the gates (left) to **Chavenage House (B)**. Take the next turning right after Chavenage House and go straight over the first crossroads.

6. On reaching a junction next to farm buildings (right) go straight on and follow the road as it soon bends right. After about half a mile, at a T-junction, turn right again in the direction of Tetbury. After about 150 yards, turn left. Follow this for about a mile to reach a junction with the A433.

7. Go right and after about 100 yards turn left, soon to climb a steep hill. You may have to get off and push for a short while. The Tetbury to Kemble railway used to run along the wooded valley below on the right. Continue past two more turnings left. Look out for Long Newnton Church and its distinctive blue sundial on your left after the second turning left.

8. At the next T-junction (with the B4014 Tetbury-Malmesbury road), turn left. After about a quarter of a mile, take the next left signposted Charlton. On reaching a T-junction (with the B4040), turn right towards Malmesbury. As you start going downhill, don't go too fast as there's a left turn coming up!

Hula-hoopers at WOMAD, Charlton Park

9. Take the first left towards Lea and Garsdon. Near the beginning of this lane on your right is **Bow-in-the-Cloud Vineyard (C)**.

10. At a crossroads, take the next right into Milbourne. Where the road bends sharp right, go straight on into a

No Through Road. Cross the main road (A429) with care to continue ahead down Blicks Hill. Take care down this hill as it can be gravelly and slippery. At the bottom of Blicks Hill, turn left up Holloway, and follow the one way system to a junction with Malmesbury High Street. Turn right to reach the Market Cross at the top of the street.

Notes:

A: **Hookshouse Pottery:** See the notes accompanying Ride 4: Tetbury.

B: **Chavenage House** is an Elizabethan manor, originally owned by Lord Seymour of Sudeley and later Sir Walter Denys of Dyrham. The house was sold to Edward Stephens of Eastington in 1587. Since then it has remained in the hands of just two families – the Stevens (as they later became) and the Lowsley-Williams families. Oliver Cromwell visited Chavenage in 1648 to persuade Colonel Nathaniel Stephens, MP for Gloucestershire, to vote for the King's impeachment. The house is open to the public on certain days, and hosts banquets, wedding receptions and corporate events. The current owner David Lowsley-Williams often leads visitor tours. For more details visit www.chavenage.com or telephone: 01666-502329.

Chavenage House

C: **Bow-in-the-Cloud Vineyard:** See the notes accompanying Ride 1: Garsdon and Charlton.

14. COTSWOLD WATER PARK

Distance:	26 miles
Pubs:	Wheatsheaf, Oaksey;
	Wild Duck, Ewen;
	Baker's Arms, Somerford Keynes;
	Horse & Groom, Charlton.
	There is a shop at Oaksey.
Map:	OS Landranger 173: Swindon & Devizes
Visiting:	Hankerton, Oaksey, Poole Keynes, Ewen,
	Upper Minety
Star-rating:	*** More challenging

The South of England's very own Lake District is great for cycling. Whilst lacking the dramatic mountain scenery of the Cumbrian lakes, the man-made Cotswold Water Park is nonetheless well worth exploring – rich in wildlife habitats and recreational opportunities. The lake side at Neigh Bridge Country Park is ideal for a picnic stop.

Route:

Looking down the High Street from the Market Cross, turn left into Oxford Street, and left again at the T-junction into Holloway. At the bottom of the hill, just after crossing the river, turn right up towards Blicks Hill. Cross the main road (A429), go though a gate and continue straight ahead. On meeting a road junction near a phone box, turn right – in effect you

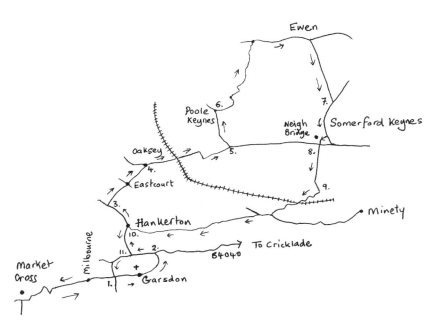

are going straight on. Continue through Milbourne, and go over Tanner's Bridge.

1. At a crossroads, go straight on and stay on the same road through Garsdon.

2. A mile of so further on, turn left at a T-junction in the direction of Charlton. Before reaching the centre of

99

the village, turn right into Vicarage Lane towards Hankerton.

3. Once through Hankerton, take the first right, with a grass triangle at the junction, to Eastcourt. On reaching a crossroads, go straight on towards **Oaksey (A)**.

Weathervane, Oaksey

Signpost and stone wall, Oaksey

4. Turn right at the roundabout in front of Oaksey post office and stores and go through the village along the B4696. The Wheatsheaf Inn (tel. 01666-577348) is on your left opposite the church. Carry on along the road over the railway line (Swindon to Kemble and Stroud).

5. After passing signs saying **Cotswold Water Park (B)** and "Cotswolds District", take the first left, signposted Poole Keynes, opposite some modern buildings.

101

6. Once in Poole Keynes, turn right at the War Memorial towards Ewen. On the outskirts of Ewen, you cross the Thames – still a shallow stream at this point – via a stone bridge. At a T-junction, turn right through Ewen, and on reaching the Wild Duck Inn (tel. 01285-770310) go right again, signposted Somerford Keynes.

Swans on the Thames at Ewen

7. On reaching a T-junction, go right through Somerford Keynes, past the Baker's Arms (tel. 01285-861298) on your right. Stay on the main road out of the village, as it bends right and soon passes the entrance (on the right) to **Neigh Bridge Country Park (C)**.

Lakeside, Neigh Bridge Country Park

8. At the crossroads next to the park's car park, go straight on, signposted to Minety. Soon you pass the entrances to two important Wiltshire Wildlife Trust nature reserves: Swillbrook Lakes, on your left, and Clattinger Farm, an area of ancient hay meadow, on the right.

9. Take the next turning right towards Minety Church, and pass over the railway (Swindon to Kemble and Stroud) at the only remaining manned railway crossing in north Wiltshire. Keep going and continue straight on at the junction with Oaksey Road. After

103

passing through Upper Minety, turn right at the T-junction, then shortly left towards Hankerton.

10. At Hankerton, turn left towards Charlton.

11. At a T-junction, turn right through Charlton, passing the Horse & Groom (tel. 01666-823904) on your right. After leaving the village, but before reaching the bottom of the hill, turn left, signposted Lea and Garsdon. At the next crossroads, turn right towards Millbourne via Tanner's Bridge. Once in Milbourne, and just by the sharp bend right, go straight ahead along a No Through Road to reach a junction with the A429. Cross the road and continue along the lane opposite down Blicks Hill to reach a T-junction at the bottom of the hill. Turn left soon to pass Malmesbury's short stay car park. At a T-junction with the High Street, turn right to reach the Market Cross.

Notes:

A: Mentioned in Domesday as Wochesie, meaning "Wocc's well watered land", **Oaksey** lies about half a mile away from the Wiltshire/ Gloucestershire border. It once had a moated castle and a small deer park, later used for steeple-chasing until 1914. A community of pacifist Christian refugees from Nazi

Germany, known as the Cotswold Bruderhof, purchased Oaksey Park Farm in 1938 and lived a self-sufficient life, sharing everything they produced or owned. They had initially settled at Ashton Fields Farm at Ashton Keynes. Soon after the outbreak of World War II, the community moved to Paraguay.

B: The **Cotswold Water Park** is the largest of its kind in the UK – bigger than the Norfolk Broads – and still growing. More than 140 lakes have been created by gravel extraction across 40 square miles. An important area for wildlife and conservation, the park offers a wealth of leisure opportunities – for water sports, cycling, walking and angling. For more information, visit www.waterpark.org

C: **Neigh Bridge Country Park:** A peaceful place to break your journey, this park lies on the western side of the Cotswold Water Park. There's a bike park next to the public toilets, a small children's play area and a few benches by the path that encircles the fishing lake (Lake 56) where you can sit and watch the waterfowl splashing about. The northern section of this pleasant circular lakeside path also takes you past the Thames. Free access all year round.

15. RODMARTON

Distance: 27 miles

Refreshments: Wheatsheaf, Crudwell;
Tavern, Kemble;
Wheatsheaf, Oaksey;
Horse & Groom, Charlton.
There is a shop at Kemble.

Maps: OS Landranger 173: Swindon & Devizes;
and 163 Cheltenham & Cirencester

Visiting: Milbourne, Garsdon, Hankerton,
Chedglow, Ashley, Culkerton,
Rodmarton, Tarlton, Kemble, Oaksey,
Eastcourt, Charlton

Star-rating: *** More challenging

A challenging ride along quiet country lanes, mainly level through beautiful Cotswold villages and hamlets, and the chance to visit two lovely gardens at Trull House and Rodmarton Manor. A short detour by foot to see the Rodmarton Long Barrow offers another opportunity to take a break in beautiful surroundings off the beaten track.

Route:

Looking down the High Street from the Market Cross,

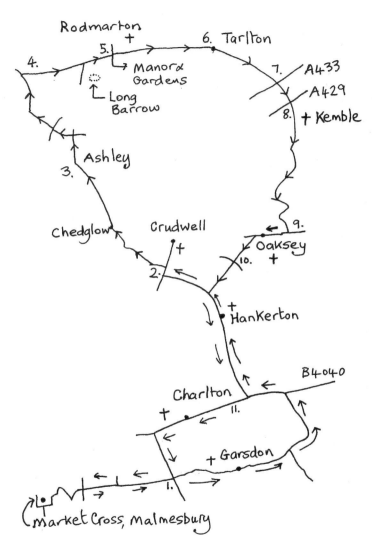

4.

Rodmarton
5.
Manor &
Gardens
Long
Barrow

6. Tarlton

7. A433
A429
8. Kemble

Ashley

3.

Chedglow

Crudwell

9.
Oaksey

2.

10.

Hankerton

B4040

Charlton

11.

Garsdon

1.

Market Cross, Malmesbury

107

turn left into Oxford Street, and left again into Holloway. At the bottom of the hill, cross over the river, then turn right up Blicks Hill. You may have to push the bike up part of this, as it is quite steep. Cross the main road, and on meeting a road junction near a phone box, continue straight on through Milbourne, and over Tanner's Bridge.

1. On reaching a crossroads, go straight on all the way through Garsdon. Ignore the turning right (Pink Lane) and continue to a T-junction. Turn left towards Charlton and, after half a mile, take the first right to Hankerton. Stay on this road until you reach a T-junction on the outskirts of Crudwell.

2. Turn right at the T-junction onto the main road (A429), and after a few hundred yards, take the first left (just before the "CRUDWELL – Drive Slowly" sign. Almost straight away go left again onto Rommel Lane. (To visit the Wheatsheaf pub (tel. 01666-577739) continue past the junction with Rommel Lane to meet the A429 again. Turn left onto this main road and you'll see the pub on your left about 150 yards down the road on your left. After your visit return to Rommel Lane.) Continue along this lane past farm buildings. At a T-junction, turn left and after about 100 yards turn right to Chedglow and Ashley. Between these two villages you soon see aircraft

hangars on the former **RAF Kemble Airfield (A)** on your right.

3. Once through Ashley, and past the duck pond, continue straight on to the hamlet of Culkerton. Turn left at the crossroads, signposted Cherington. On reaching a main road (A433), cross the road with care to follow the lane straight ahead, again signposted to Cherington. Soon the lane bends right through a strip of woodland.

4. At the next junction turn right. After 1½ miles a right turning will take you to **Trull House Gardens (B)**. (If you detour to visit these gardens, return to this junction afterwards.) Shortly after passing this turning to Trull House Gardens, watch out for a sign to Rodmarton Long Barrow (right), a five minute walk away from the road. On reaching a cattle grid and drive going left, follow the lane as it bends right, and take the first left to Rodmarton.

5. At a T-junction just before the village, turn right to visit **Rodmarton Manor Gardens (C)**, whose entrance you will soon see on the left. On leaving turn right out of the entrance and go right again through Rodmarton village. If not visiting Rodmarton Manor, go left at the T-junction and almost immediately right into the village, past St Peter's Church on your left.

Continue along the road as it bends round to the right towards Tarlton.

Rodmarton Long Barrow

6. Once past the Tarlton water tower, follow the road as it bends right, and take the road signposted Kemble out of the village.

7. As you pedal gently downhill for almost two miles, almost as far as Kemble, the vast prairie-like landscape seems barely recognisable as Cotswolds country, resembling rather East Anglia perhaps. Cross over the main road (A433), and continue along the lane straight ahead, soon to dip underneath the railway line, finally into **Kemble (D)**. After passing the shop on the right, a turning on the right takes you to the Tavern Inn (tel. 01285-770216) on the other side of the railway line.

Kemble Railway Station, opened in 1882

8. On reaching a T-junction with the A429, Cirencester to Chippenham road, go right and immediately left into the northern part of the village. Go right into West Lane, signposted Oaksey and Crudwell, and then take the first left. Follow the road as it passes the church and Kemble House, over the railway line and soon through the hamlet of Kemble Wick towards Oaksey. Continue along the sunken lane flanked by

high hedgerows on each side for a mile or so. Ignore the sign to Poole Keynes.

9. On reaching a T-junction, turn right through Oaksey – the Wheatsheaf Inn (tel. 01666-577348) is on your right opposite the church – and then take the left turn opposite the post office and stores towards Eastcourt and Malmesbury.

10. On reaching Eastcourt, turn right and then almost immediately left towards Hankerton. At the next T-junction, turn left towards Hankerton. Go through the village, ignore signs to left and right, and stay on this road towards Charlton.

11. At the next T-junction, turn right. Go through Charlton, past the Horse & Groom (tel. 01666-823904) on your right, and take the first left out of the village, signed to Lea and Garsdon. Take the first right towards Milbourne and go over Tanner's Bridge. Once in Milbourne, and where the road bends sharp right, continue straight ahead along a No Through Road to reach a T-junction with the A429. Cross the road and pick up the lane opposite down Blicks Hill (can be gravelly and slippery) to reach a T-junction at the bottom. Turn left into Holloway and follow the road past the short-stay car park to a junction with Malmesbury High Street. Turn right soon to reach the Market Cross.

Spring lambs, Milbourne

Notes:

A: Formerly the home of the famous Red Arrows aerobatic team, **Kemble Airfield** was used by both the RAF and the USAF over half a century. An RAF base from 1938, it became a civilian airfield in the 1990s, a role it continues to play despite talk of covering it with housing. On the 40th anniversary of their formation, the Red Arrows returned to give a display at Kemble Air Day 2004. The Bristol Aero Collection, an aviation museum is housed there, and a café open to the public. The main entrance is off the A429 between Crudwell and Kemble.

B: **Trull House Gardens** are spread over eight acres and feature a sunken lily pond, a rockery, wild garden and walled gardens, lawns, trees and shrubs. Home-grown plants for sale, and other produce as available. For opening times and more information visit www.trullhouse.co.uk

Garden-loving peacock butterfly, Trull House Gardens

C: **Rodmarton Manor** has been described as the last great country house built in England, constructed between 1909 and 1926 by Ernest Barnsley, of nearby Sapperton, for the Hon. Claud Biddulph. A leading light in the Arts and Crafts Movement, Barnsley also masterminded the furnishing of the house by local craftsmen. The eight-acre Rodmarton Manor Gardens, famed for its snowdrops and topiary, features a series of themed "outdoor rooms" with far-reaching views towards the Wiltshire Downs. For opening times and other details, please visit www.rodmarton-manor.co.uk or telephone 01285-841253

D: **Kemble:** The village railway station was completed by the GWR in 1872, many years after Isambard Kingdom Brunel conducted protracted negotiations with the local squire, Robert Gordon of Kemble House. Gordon finally accepted £7,500 in compensation for the railway going near his house, but insisted on a 415-yard tunnel being built to protect his views. All Saints Church, Kemble contains some spectacular stained glass installed in 2000. Incumbent vicars going back to the 1300s are named in the porch, although the first church is thought to have been built in 682 after Cedwalla, King of Wessex, granted land at Kemble to Aldhelm, the Abbot of Malmesbury. In the churchyard grows the great yew, considered to be Anglo-Saxon in origin, in whose trunk a new yew tree is growing. Kemble House, a 17th century stone-built manor, is next door. For more information about Garsdon and Charlton, see the notes accompanying Ride 1, and about Oaksey, see the notes accompanying Ride 14: Cotswold Water Park.

16. LYDIARD PARK

Distance:	31 miles
Refreshments:	Royal George, Purton;
	Bolingbroke Arms, Greatfield;
	The Sun Inn, Lydiard Millicent;
	The Rose & Crown, Lea.
	Café and picnic areas at Lydiard Park
Map:	OS Landranger 173: Swindon & Devizes
Visiting:	Milbourne, Garsdon, Braydon, Purton,
	Lydiard Millicent, Somerford Common,
	Cleverton and Lea
Star-rating:	*** More challenging

Set off early for a grand day out to visit the wonderful parkland and former stately home of the St John family at Lydiard Park, three miles west of Swindon centre. Ensure you've acquired the necessary fitness, stamina and road skills to tackle a ride of this length and challenge. There are a few hills to climb – the steepest is Pavenhill, west of Purton. If you are well-prepared, this route promises an ideal outing for a spring or summer Sunday or Bank Holiday Monday when roads west of Swindon are likely to be less busy than at other times.

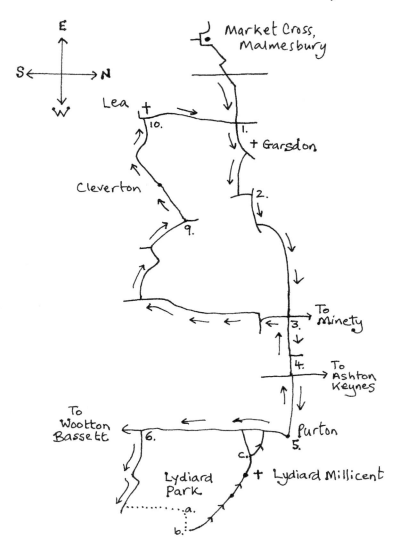

E
S ← → N
W

Market Cross, Malmesbury

Lea ✝ 10.
1. ✝ Garsdon
Cleverton
2.
9.
To Minety
3.
4. To Ashton Keynes
To Wootton Bassett ← 6.
Purton
5.
c.
Lydiard Park
✝ Lydiard Millicent
a.
b.

Route:

Looking down High Street, Malmesbury from the Market Cross, turn left into Oxford Street, and left again into Holloway. Just after crossing the bridge over the Avon, turn right up Blicks Hill. You may have to push the bike up part of this, as it is quite steep. Cross the A429 with care, and continue ahead through a gate along a narrow country lane. Go straight on at the road junction near a phone box. Continue through Milbourne, and cross over Tanner's Bridge.

1. At a crossroads, go straight on towards Garsdon. Once past the church on your left, turn right at the next junction, signposted Brinkworth and Purton, along Park Lane, where lovely views open up on each side. Keep going for about two miles.

2. On reaching a T-junction, turn left, and then almost straight away turn right signposted Purton. Here you are going along the southern edge of Braydon Wood. Carry on for about half a mile with trees on each side of the road. Take the next left turning just before a dip in the road, keeping the woodland on your left and, on your right a field, beyond a hedge. Keep going for about three miles to reach a crossroads.

3. Go straight on past a Purton Parish stone marker by the signpost on your left. Keep going for about a mile.

Cowslips blooming on the way to Purton

4. On reaching a T-junction (and another Purton Parish stone on your left) turn right (in effect you are going straight on). After nearly a mile, at the next crossroads (signposted Ashton Keynes left and Wootton Bassett right) continue straight ahead towards Purton, which you will soon see perched on the hill ahead of you. Climb the hill (called Pavenhill) to enter the outskirts of Purton. Pass the Royal George Inn (tel. 01793-770378) on the right.

5. At the first mini-roundabout, turn right up a gently sloping hill towards Wootton Bassett and stay on this road for about three miles through Restrop and Greatfield into Hook.

6. After passing the Bolingbroke Arms (tel. 01793-852357) on your left, take the next left signposted Lydiard Park. There are lovely views over to the right towards the Wiltshire Downs. Take care over the cattle grids and note the passing spaces along this single track lane. After nearly two miles, turn left into **Lydiard Park (A)** opposite the signpost. Once in the

Lydiard House in winter

park, you will soon reach a mini-roundabout. The visitor centre and café are on your left, the picnic area to your right. There is cycle parking near the children's playground and behind the café. **Lydiard House (B)** and the newly restored walled garden are further along the main drive.

There are two ways of getting back to Purton to start the return leg to Malmesbury: the way you came (the directions continue below) or an *alternative route via Lydiard Millicent** described at the end of the main route directions.

Mares and foals, Lydiard Park

The way you came: Exit the park the way you entered it and turn right. At the T-junction, turn right, signposted Purton and continue to the mini-roundabout at Purton mentioned at the start of point 5. Turn left at the mini-roundabout aiming for Pavenhill soon to pass the Royal George pub again (on your left), and start your descent of the hill.

7. After the road has levelled out, go straight on at the crossroads (mentioned at point 4), signposted Garsdon. After a mile, turn left (in effect straight on) past Braydon Manor on your left along a road lacking a signpost, and continue for about a mile. At the next crossroads, turn left towards Brinkworth. At the next T-junction, turn right then almost immediately left, signposted Brinkworth, through **Somerford Common (C)**.

8. Keep going for about a mile, gently downhill. At the bottom of the hill, turn right, signposted Hulberts Green and stay on the road for about a mile and a half past Hulberts Green Riding Centre and Hulberts Green Farm. Ignore the next turning left (signposted Malmesbury and Brinkworth) and instead follow the road as it bends right, signposted to Charlton. As you start pedalling uphill along a gentle incline, passing farms on either side, you should see the top of Sundays Hill away to your right.

Lane near Hulberts Green, looking west towards Cleverton

9. When you approach the brow of the hill, prepare to turn left along an single track lane (not signposted) which takes you towards Cleverton. After turning left onto the lane, you should see pleasant far-reaching views on either side as you begin a gradual descent. Continue for about two miles to reach Cleverton. Leave the hamlet via the next turning right signposted to Lea, and carry on along this single track lane for about two miles.

10. At a T-junction, by Lea Church, turn right to pass the Rose & Crown (tel. 01666-824344) and continue right through the village, passing the primary school on your left. At the top of a hill, turn left at a crossroads, signposted Malmesbury and Milbourne. In Milbourne, where the road bends sharp right, go straight on along a No Through Road. Go through the gate at the end of it, cross the A429 Chippenham to Cirencester road with care and continue along the lane ahead of you: Blicks Hill. The lane soon descends quite steeply to a T-junction. Turn left up Holloway, and follow the road past Malmesbury Town Hall, the short stay car park to reach a T-junction with the High Street. Turn right to return to the Market Cross.

* Alternative route via Lydiard Millicent:

a) From the visitor centre and café, continue along the drive to pass between the Stables and the Lydiard Park Conference Centre to reach a car park. Turn right along another drive soon to reach the Hay Lane (west Swindon) entrance/exit to the park.

b) Turn left and, almost straight away, take the footpath and cycleway (left) that passes behind houses. After about ¼ of a mile, you reach a junction. Turn left (onto Tewkesbury Way) soon to reach a roundabout. Take the first exit off the roundabout, signposted Lydiard Millicent, and keep going gently uphill. Go straight across a mini-roundabout. Note the traffic calming system through Lydiard Millicent, and observe the "Give Way" signs. Pass the Sun Inn (tel.

01793-770425) on your left. At the next mini-roundabout bear left towards Wootton Bassett, passing the church.

c) After passing a road on the right called The Beeches, then further on a 30 mph sign and a farm entrance on your right, take the next turning right into Bagbury Lane. Continue to a T-junction and then turn right towards Purton. Proceed with extra care here because of bends in the road. At the mini-roundabout in Purton (mentioned at the start of point 5), take the first exit left, aiming for Pavenhill soon to pass the Royal George pub again and start your descent of the hill. Continue as described above from the start of point 7 to return to Malmesbury.

Notes:

A: Originally a medieval deer park, **Lydiard Park** now extends to around 260 acres of formal parkland, pasture, woods, lake, play and picnic areas – linked by a network of well-maintained, easily navigable foot and cycle paths. In 2005, work began on a £5 million landscape restoration project, supported by the Heritage Lottery Fund. Access to the park, owned and run by Swindon Borough Council, is free of charge and it is open daily until dusk. For more information visit www.lydiardpark.org or pick up a leaflet from the visitor centre and café or from local tourist information offices.

B: **Lydiard House,** at the heart of Lydiard Park, lies about three miles west from the centre of Swindon. It was re-modelled in about 1743 in the Palladian style for members of the St John family which owned the park from the 15th century to the early 20th century. In 1712, Henry St John was granted the title of Viscount Bolingbroke, whose son married Lady Diana Spencer, who shared an ancestry (and apparently a certain likeness) with Diana, Princess of Wales. For details of opening times and entry charges for the house and walled garden, visit www.lydiardpark.org

C: **Somerford Common:** see the notes accompanying Ride 9: Callow Hill.

HIGHLIGHTS OF THE YEAR

MAY:
Tetbury Woolsack Races – Whit Bank Holiday Monday
Badminton Horse Trials
Beaufort Polo Club – weekend matches May to September
Wild flowers – Distillery Meadows, near Minety (May to July)

JULY:
World of Music, Arts and Dance (WOMAD) Festival, Charlton Park
Sherston Boules Festival

AUGUST:
Somerford Show
Malmesbury Carnival – last fortnight in August/ first week September

BIBLIOGRAPHY

Badminton

The Badminton Tradition – Barry Campbell (Michael Joseph, 1978)

Memoirs – The Duke of Beaufort (Country Life Books, 1981)

Brokenborough

Almost A Fairy Story. A History of Easton Grey House – Peter Saunders

Castle Combe
The Buildings of England: Wiltshire – Nikolaus Pevsner, revised by Bridget Cherry (Penguin Books, 1975)

Wiltshire Forefathers – June Badeni (1982)

Garsdon & Charlton, Tetbury

Charlton Park – A Short History – Kate Mason (1996)

Didmarton

The Secret Servant: The Life of Sir Stewart Menzies: Churchill's Spymaster – Anthony Cave Brown (Michael Joseph, 1988)

The Two of Us: My Life with John Thaw – Sheila Hancock (Bloomsbury, 2004)

The Making of Pride and Prejudice – Sue Birtwhistle & Susie Conklin (Penguin, 2003)

Tin Tabernacles – Corrugated Iron Mission Halls, Churches and Chapels of Britain – Ian Smith (Camrose Organisation, 2004)

Minety, The Somerfords, Cotswold Water Park

An Acre of England – L.J. Manners (Unwin Brothers Ltd, 1977)

The Malmesbury Branch – Mike Fenton (Wild Swan Publications, 1990)

Wiltshire Railway Stations – Mike Oakley (The Dovecote Press Ltd, 2004)

The Wiltshire Cotswolds – Ken Watts (Hobnob Press, 2007)

Callow Hill

Brinkworth with Grittenham – Graham Greener and Joanna Clothier (The Brinkworth Heritage Society, 2000)